"A capacious and mind-opening experience awaits within."
—*Publishers Weekly*, starred review

"This brief but incisive reflection on the history of voting among African-Americans takes the form of a classic personal essay: light and conversational, circling its subject in a deliberately meandering style that ends up revealing more than a frontal attack might have." —*The New Yorker*

"*Blackballed* is timely and essential. Recent police killings of black boys and men have once again pushed race to the forefront of public awareness, and Darryl Pinckney's slender volume asks that we pause and look deeper—into the past, into the current state of our democracy and into 'what black means now.'" —*The Washington Post*

"[This] slim book ... offers a brisk history of black voting rights. It covers a lot of ground, surveying the trajectory of the civil-rights movement, musing on the influence of social media in the 2012 election, and describing the Supreme Court's 2013 decision overturning a key section of the Voting Rights Act."
—*The Nation*

"Part memoir, part historical reflection, all political: there's something for everyone." —*Real Simple*

"As young Americans take to the streets to say black lives matter, they're often told to vote. While voting is important, it's also important to remember how black political representation has been chipped away by voter ID laws, gerrymandering and felon disenfranchisement. *Blackballed* addresses the struggle for voting rights and for racial equality more broadly, drawing on Pinckney's own experiences and writings of civil rights leaders to create a complicated picture of black political identity."
—*NPR Code Switch*

"A slim volume of two essays that challenge the very notion of a "post-racial" America... Particularly incisive on the process of marketing black stereotypes... Not a manifesto but a thoughtful examination of ideas." —*Kirkus Reviews*

"Entertaining and enlightening... Pinckney enlivens his sketches of historical figures with snapshots of the most dramatic moments in their lives and examinations of the deeper political contexts in which those moments unfolded.... Like [Jess] Row and [Claudia] Rankine, Pinckney matches narrative form to function in clever and striking ways." —*Public Books*

"Any reader familiar with the essays of Darryl Pinckney—in *The New York Review of Books*, for instance, or 2014's *Blackballed*, a memoir/political dissection of efforts to suppress African American voter rights—knows that his writing is consistently informed by intellectual savvy and sharp wit. His fusion of the personal and the political makes him a peerless witness and participant, and lends his voice a weight and force that never comes at the expense of style or grace." —*SFGate*

"*Blackballed* is a masterfully-crafted study of American democracy and the changing role of the black vote within it, from Reconstruction to the election of Barack Obama. It is insightful, personal, informative, and remarkably timely. The book not only speaks to current questions about race within the social and political arenas, but to broader issues of the health and legitimacy of a democracy in which some voices are kept from entering the dialogue. *Blackballed* is one of those special works that effortlessly transports readers to another time while subtly drawing thematic ties to the present day. One leaves the experience not only appreciating the work done by generations past, but contemplating one's own role in the historical arc."
—*Challenges to Democracy* blog

Blackballed

The Black Vote and US Democracy

Blackballed

The Black Vote and US Democracy

Darryl Pinckney

NEW YORK REVIEW BOOKS

New York

THIS IS A NEW YORK REVIEW BOOK

PUBLISHED BY THE NEW YORK REVIEW OF BOOKS

Published by The New York Review of Books, 435 Hudson Street, Suite 300, New York, NY 10014
www.nyrb.com

The Library of Congress has catalogued the hardcover edition of this book as follows:

Pinckney, Darryl, 1953–
Blackballed : the Black vote and US democracy / by Darryl Pinckney.
   pages cm
   ISBN 978-1-59017-769-3 (hardback : alkaline paper)
   1. African Americans—Suffrage—History. 2. Voting—United States—History. 3. Political participation—United States—History. 4. Elections—United States—History. 5. African Americans—Politics
and government. 6. African Americans—Civil rights—History. 7. Pinckney, Darryl, 1953—Childhood
and youth. 8. Democracy—United States—History. 9. United States—Politics and government. 10.
United States—Race relations—Political aspects. I. Title.
JK1924.P65 2014
324.6'208996073—dc23
                              2014019161

ISBN 978-1-68137-559-5 Paperback

Also available as an electronic book; 978-1-68137-560-1

Printed in the United States of America on acid-free paper.

1 3 5 7 9 10 8 6 4 2

For my brother-in-law,
Wayne Withers

Contents

Acknowledgments

I THANK ROBERT SILVERS for the chance to give in 2012 the lecture named for him at the New York Public Library—the title essay of this book is based on that lecture—and for opening the pages of *The New York Review of Books* to me all those many years ago. I want also to thank Michael Shae for his patience with me and his careful reading of this work.

BLACKBALLED:
THE BLACK VOTE AND US DEMOCRACY

"I WAS WRONG," I remember my father saying in 2004. Kerry's exit polls had shown him ahead in Florida and Ohio, but by ten thirty everyone I knew had gone home. Bush won, which meant that the Republicans controlled the White House, both houses of Congress, the Supreme Court, and television news. "It's their world," my mother said. She said that the morning after the election instead of the news she had coffee in front of reruns of *Little House on the Prairie*, because at least in that world the bad were punished.

My father often lectured me on black history. He once told me that had he not left Georgia he would have ended up dead. Truman was the last Democratic candidate to win the presidency without the South. My father forgot that Truman took Georgia. Then, too, Truman in 1948, like Johnson in 1964, won Texas, Florida, and

the Upper South. But my father did not like to be interrupted. The Dixiecrats went to the Republican Party
and said that they would be the party to contain the
blacks, as he put it. Since 1968, the Republicans had
gone into every election with the advantage of not need-
ing to campaign in the South, of knowing that they had
136 electoral votes or thereabouts straight off the bat.
There were few voting stations in districts where blacks
lived, meaning the lines to vote were long, it could take
hours, and often people were given hell for missing
work. In other words, they didn't have to steal the election, because it was nearly fixed to begin with. "Kerry
did well, considering how rigged democracy is in the
US," my father said.

I had a folder of printed-out articles about the previous election, how there had been more votes cast in
Cuyahoga County, Ohio, than there were voters registered, for instance. But on that visit home to Indianapolis, I noticed that the plastic on the DVD of *Fahrenheit
911*, Michael Moore's 2004 documentary about the
Bush administration's corruption that I'd given my parents, had not been unwrapped. I'd especially wanted
them to see the opening scene of the joint congressional
session that certified the 2000 election results. For
members of the House to object officially, they had to
have the signed support of at least one senator. In the

scene, Black Caucus member after Black Caucus member comes forward to lament that "the Senate is missing." Even Ted Kennedy remained seated.

I am glad that my father and mother lived long enough to fill out their absentee ballots and to see Barack Obama win. The 106-year-old black voter whom the president-elect made special mention of as someone who had to wait in line a long time before she could cast her ballot was my grandparents' next-door neighbor in Atlanta, and her daughter and my mother were college roommates. She was also the grandmother of noted Harvard sociologist Lawrence Bobo, I said. My mother became her old self long enough to fix me that look. "You're such a snob," she said. My parents watched the Inauguration in matching wheelchairs and then they went downhill further and died, side by side, as they had done most things through the sixty-three years of their marriage.

I.

White violence against blacks had gone unpunished for the most part during Reconstruction, when black candidates, black voting officials, and black voters were beaten or killed by gangs of hooded vigilantes. Crops and farms were burned; there was a strong correlation between voting and landownership among blacks during Reconstruction. Many whites just could not abide the fact of black people owning property like white people. The Compromise of 1877 by which Rutherford B. Hayes and his whiskers became president ended Reconstruction. Hayes withdrew federal troops from the former states of the Confederacy while white supremacists reclaimed their power, driving blacks from office and from the voting rolls, subjecting them to political persecution.

The first section of the Fifteenth Amendment states that the federal government cannot—and that state governments also cannot—deny United States citizens the right to vote based on race, color, or "previous condition of servitude." The second and final clause gives Congress the power to enforce the first provision. However, the purposely spare wording of the amendment does not define universal suffrage or establish uniform requirements for voting. After the Civil War, Republicans who supported blacks voting in the South opposed the Chinese having the vote in California. Moreover, the Fifteenth Amendment does not rule out property requirements, poll taxes, or literacy tests, means by which European immigrants and the white poor as well as free blacks had been excluded from the rolls, historically, depending on which state they lived in.

I was surprised some years ago to read in a book about Promised Land, South Carolina, a community founded in 1870 by freedmen, including a great-great-grandfather of mine, that these freedmen continued to vote after Reconstruction. It was "a community of literate preachers, teachers, carpenters, and subsistence farmers who paid their poll tax regularly and kept their receipts."[1] In one story about elections in the early 1880s, a white sheriff warned the Red Shirts, a white paramilitary group, that the blacks in Promised Land had a reputation for using their Winchesters and shotguns. Black men walked three miles to the polls at the post office in the next town. They went in groups, the better to protect themselves. There was one box for ballots cast by blacks, a separate box for those of whites.

Promised Land survived, perhaps because it was an overlooked, isolated Negro world. In the 1890s, the Democratic Party and state legislatures throughout the former Confederacy established all-white primaries from which black voters were banned. Black people were in effect excluded from the electoral process. They were a subdued population, politically. A black person could be killed or abducted for no reason on the way home from church and the crime never investigated.

Throughout the South as states rejoined the Union state legislatures passed laws that disfranchised black people. The federal government did not help; neither did the federal courts or even the Supreme Court, insisting that black people had a remedy in that they could file suit in their states. But because blacks were barred from juries and election boards, their cases were never heard. Southern congressional power needed unfairness: the number of representatives southern states were entitled to was determined by their total populations. However, those unlikely to support the Democrats were kept from voting. In 1904, though 782,509 black people represented 58 percent of South Carolina's population, only 25,433 blacks voted.

Sojourner Truth had her reasons for opposing the Fifteenth Amendment. She didn't want having the vote to give black men power over black women, who had, in theory, only just thrown off the white man's yoke. At the turn of the twentieth century, Susan B. Anthony and Elizabeth Cady Stanton were enraged that black men had the vote while white women did not. Middle-class white women offered their vote as a counterweight to the vote of the poor and of working-class, naturalized Americans. But Frederick Douglass—and the black novelist Frances E. W. Harper—concluded that if the black race had no rights, then the women's struggle would be meaningless for black women. "When women are hunted down because they are women, then they will have an urgency to obtain the ballot equal to our own," Douglass said. Black women were hunted down not because they were women but because they were black, he added. But many black women continued to agitate for women's suffrage.

The Ku Klux Klan reemerged after thousands of black women tried to vote in 1920. Whites marched through black neighborhoods in Jacksonville, Florida, but in spite of the campaign of intimidation, blacks stood in lines to vote. White registrars resorted to delaying tactics and managed to keep an estimated four thousand blacks in the city from voting. In Ocoee, in central Florida, a black owner of an orange grove, resented by whites because of his prosperity, was lynched by a mob when he tried to vote. The racial violence that continued in the town left fifty-six black people dead. To add minorities to the vote was not a goal most politicians were in favor of. As Alexander Keyssar notes in *The Right to Vote: The Contested History of Democracy in the United States* (2000), elections were also rituals of white supremacy and racist rhetoric was an important feature of campaigns. Anti-lynching legislation routinely failed in Congress throughout the 1920s.

Blacks in the South did not get much out of the New Deal, as Ira Katznelson shows in *When Affirmative Action Was White: An Untold History of Racial Inequality in Twentieth-Century America* (2005). For instance, the Social Security Act of 1935 represented an unheard-of opportunity for blacks, yet "fully 65 percent of African Americans fell outside the reach of the new program; between 70 and 80 percent in different parts of the South," because people who had been farmworkers and domestic help were ineligible to receive benefits. Without such "occupational disabilities" as part of the legislation, "the program's inclusive and national structure would have powerfully undermined the racialized, low-wage economy" on which Jim Crow stood. Franklin Roosevelt had had to make concessions to southern congressmen in order to get his legislative program passed. Moreover, the federal government left the running of New Deal programs to the states, which in the South resulted in what Katznelson calls "policy apartheid."

Nevertheless, because of limited gains under the New Deal, black voters in the northern cities began in 1936 to move away from the party of Lincoln. But for blacks to vote Democratic in the North did not mean the same thing as it did in the South. In 1937, in *Breedlove* v. *Suttles*, the Supreme Court upheld the local and state election poll tax in Georgia. Southern filibusters in the Senate defeated attempts to pass legislation making the poll tax illegal. Even when proposals were before Congress in 1943 concerning the reintegration of military veterans, southern politicians made sure that they were in control of the legislation and could guard the old order.

White supremacy still ruled the South, but in 1944 in *Smith* v. *Allwright* the Supreme Court found the white-only primaries of the Democratic Party of Texas unconstitutional, reversing previous Court decisions. Keyssar points out that among the reasons for the shift was the changed composition of the Court. Roosevelt's New Deal appointees were willing "to extend federal authority over state voting laws." Previous rulings had held that primaries were not elections within the meaning of the Constitution and also that political parties were voluntary or private organizations and therefore their membership requirements did not violate the Fourteenth and Fifteenth Amendments. However, the Court decided that political parties were not private but rather agencies of the states, being regulated by state statutes.

In spite of *To Secure These Rights*, the 1947 report of Truman's Committee on Civil Rights that recommended desegregation in public facilities, education, and the military, some of Atlanta's blacks, among them Martin Luther King Sr., frustrated by the domination of segregationists within the Democratic Party in the South, formed a group to take blacks back to the Republican Party. However, these black voters were in the big cities, like Condoleezza Rice's parents, who were Republicans in Birmingham, Alabama. Black churches and black colleges were self-contained communities that afforded some protection for blacks, especially in a city like Atlanta where there was a significant black middle class, in part because of the number of black educational institutions there. However, voting was not a part of small-town and rural life for blacks in the Deep South.

Civil rights may have been one of the planks at the 1948 Democratic convention, but Strom Thurmond's rebellion was aided by the Communist witch hunt. Liberals became timid. "Not until 1954, when Republicans controlled the White House, the Senate, and the House of Representatives, and southern Democrats finally lost their ability to mold legislation, were the occupational exclusions that had kept the large majority of blacks out of the Social Security system eliminated," Katznelson observes.

"Give us the ballot," Martin Luther King Jr. said in a Prayer Pilgrimage March on Washington in 1957. The Civil Rights Act of 1957 contained a provision whereby the Justice Department could sue those who sought to intimidate or coerce voters, but it was not enforced. In France, everyone pretends to have been in the Resistance, and no one was a collaborator. So, too, in retrospect everyone participated in the civil rights movement. But there was nothing widespread about it at the time of the Montgomery bus boycott. Black ministers and black educators protected their institutions by keeping away from trouble.

To be a race leader or the head of a civil rights group had become a middle-class career. Ralph Bunche, who as undersecretary-general of the United Nations shared the Nobel Peace Prize in 1950 for his part in negotiating an end to the first Arab-Israeli war, wrote four memoranda for Gunnar Myrdal in 1940 when Myrdal was at work on his monumental study of race in America, *An American Dilemma* (1944). In the memorandum on black leadership, Bunche looked back to Frederick Douglass, who believed that the future of black people would be made secure by the exercise of the franchise.

Black leaders split over what was more essential to black freedom. W. E. B. Du Bois and the National Association for the Advancement of Colored People (NAACP), founded in New York in 1909, championed political rights, and Booker T. Washington, the founder of the Tuskegee Institute in Alabama, the best-known vocational school in the South, and the president of the National Negro Business League, cautioned blacks to cast down their buckets where they were and to live with segregation. Region and class did not necessarily dictate which side blacks took, a debate that shaped strategies for freedom among blacks well into the 1970s.

Bunche accepted the philosophies of Washington and Du Bois both, praising Washington for getting black people through hard times after their political dreams had been destroyed, and then praising Du Bois for vigorously redefining the importance of civil liberties. But the mass of Negroes was remote from the black leaders of the professional class, and because of the racial mores of the country, Bunche said,

> it is beyond the conceptions of both Negroes and whites that, for instance, there should ever be a Negro president in this country. Only a very emancipated few can think in terms of Negro leadership attaining the exalted heights of a position in the cabinet, or on the Supreme Court, or a general in the Army, or even a Senator.

James Baldwin said that Martin Luther King Jr. was the first Negro leader to say to whites what he said to blacks. Before King, the Negro leader had only been at the bargaining table to force from his adversary what he could get: new schools or new jobs. "He was invested with very little power because the Negro vote had so little power." What concessions the Negro leader carried away were won with the tacit understanding that blacks would not agitate for more. That was why both whites and blacks found King dangerous, because he genuinely believed in the mission to prepare blacks for first-class citizenship. People seldom give their power away, Baldwin noted. "Forces beyond their control take their power from them."

King understood that American officials couldn't call for free elections in Europe when there weren't free elections in Alabama or Georgia. The civil rights movement was going to complete the process of democratization in the US. However, King warned in *Stride Toward Freedom* (1958), his account of the Montgomery bus boycott, that underhanded methods by white officials were not the only barriers that kept blacks from voting. Blacks themselves were slow to exercise their voting privileges, even when the polls were open to them. Black leaders had to make a concerted effort to arouse their people. Apathy was not only a moral failing; it was political suicide.

Septima Clark relates in her autobiography, *Echo in My Soul* (1962), her work with the Citizenship Education Program, which was designed to teach black people to read and write as part of their preparation to register to vote. In the late 1950s, the group held workshops in different communities, from East Texas to Virginia, looking to train people in each place who could, in turn, train others in their towns, teach them how to be comfortable fulfilling their civic duties. However, because the Citizenship Education Program was associated with Clark's Highlander Folk School in Tennessee, it was not entirely trusted by blacks. Even though Rosa Parks had been trained at Highlander, it had long been an experiment in coalitions, held integrated political meetings, and as such was suspected of being a Communist Party front.

Eventually, the Highlander Folk School closed and the Citizenship Education Program, paid for by a grant from the Marshall Field Foundation, was transferred to King's Southern Christian Leadership Council (SCLC). In spite of great opposition, the Citizenship Education Program trained enough people to open schools in eighteen Georgia counties. Some nine thousand blacks were able to answer Georgia's notorious "thirty questions" on its literacy tests and joined the roll of voters in 1961, before passage of any voting rights legislation.

In 1961, the safest way for a civil rights worker to travel in Mississippi, Congressman John Lewis tells us in his memoir, *Walking with the Wind* (1998), was to take a car on the back roads at night at one hundred miles an hour with no headlights on. Lewis, an Ala-

bama Bible college student, would go to jail that summer, along with James Farmer, the founder of the
Congress of Racial Equality (CORE). Farmer recalls in
*Lay Bare the Heart: An Autobiography of the Civil
Rights Movement* (1985) that he was afraid to go to
Mississippi with the Freedom Riders he'd recruited. He
came to see them off at the bus station with the many
reasons he could not leave Chicago. But the terrified expression of one young woman shamed him into getting
on the bus. They would barely escape with their lives.

What comes across in these memoirs is how dangerous those days were. Blacks known merely to talk about
voting in certain towns in Alabama or Mississippi could
get fired or have their businesses wrecked. Back then
there was no guarantee about how things would turn
out, no experience of American politics that could reas-
sure black people that justice would prevail. Police dogs,
fire hoses, mass arrests, beatings, assassinations—Anne
Moody's stoic autobiography, *Coming of Age in Mississippi* (1968), reminds us that the violence meted out to
civil rights demonstrators was not new. Moody remembers that after Emmett Till was murdered in Mississippi
in 1955 for having supposedly whistled at a white
woman, she was convinced that she, too, would be
killed, just because she was a black child. Moody tells
how in the early 1960s her family all but hid from her,

DARRYL PINCKNEY

so fearful were they of reprisals because of the trouble
she was stirring up as a volunteer registrar in a nearby
county.

King knew his Thoreau: "For it matters not how small
the beginning may seem to be." Less than one percent
of Alabama's eligible black voters were registered when
a local group, the Dallas County Voters League, first
tried to add black names to the rolls in the late 1950s. In
1963, registrars from the Student Nonviolent Coordi-
nating Committee (SNCC) joined the effort and were
attacked by whites. The all-white school board in Dallas County, of which Selma is the county seat, fired
thirty-two black teachers who'd applied to register.
Mass meetings increased in size and frequency. The police attacked again, their aggression captured on the
evening news. John F. Kennedy, who had called Coretta
Scott King when her husband was jailed in 1960, proposed a civil rights bill and addressed the nation, saying
that the Constitution's intent was clear. King had noted
that the black vote in the South contributed to Kennedy's
margin of victory in states such as South Carolina.

In the fall of 1963, the Klan reacted to the March on
Washington for Jobs and Freedom by killing four black
girls in a church bombing in Birmingham, Alabama.

Black students began sit-in demonstrations at Selma lunch counters. Hundreds were arrested and hundreds more the following month when blacks converged on the voter registration office. Even after President Lyndon Johnson signed the Civil Rights Act in the summer of 1964 that made segregation illegal, Selma's sheriff continued to arrest blacks who tried to register. Malcolm X urged blacks to hold back their votes as if they were bullets and not to use them until their target was in sight. The turmoil in the South was answered by a summer of black unrest in northern cities.

The integrated Mississippi Democratic Freedom Party challenged the legitimacy of the white-only delegation at the Democratic Party's national convention in 1964, but Johnson was unwilling to risk offending the white vote in the South and refused to support reform. The Democrats won the election by a wide margin, not in small part because of the tender feelings that remained following Kennedy's assassination, but also because the black vote nationally offset the widespread defection of white southerners to Goldwater and the Republicans.

"Give us the ballot," King said again in Selma to a packed chapel, violating a court injunction against more than three blacks congregating in public at any one time. President Johnson hadn't been greatly interested in a voting rights act when King visited the White House on his way home from receiving the Nobel Peace Prize in December 1964. In February 1965, shortly after Malcolm X was gunned down in New York, a young man who'd been part of a march in Marion, Alabama, on behalf of a civil rights worker held in the town jail was shot while trying to shield his grandmother from police violence. He died a week later. A grand jury refused to indict the state trooper who'd fired on him at close range. The SCLC organized a march from Selma to Montgomery in response.

In early March, some six hundred civil rights protesters tried to cross over the Alabama River just outside Selma. They were met by state troopers on the Edmund Pettus Bridge. The troopers, some on horseback, attacked the protesters with tear gas, billy clubs, and bullwhips. ABC interrupted its regular programming that night to show footage of the brutality. Two days later King led a second, largely symbolic march of 2,500 to the Edmund Pettus Bridge for prayer. But that evening three white ministers were attacked, one of whom died of his injuries. A judge upheld the First Amendment rights of the protestors and at the end of the month several thousand set off from Selma behind King, through Lowndes County, notorious as a "totalitarian state" that was 81 percent black but where no blacks were registered to vote.

Four days later an estimated crowd of 25,000 gathered at the statehouse steps in Montgomery, the former capital of the Confederacy, to hear King ask and answer: How long? Not long. But that night, a white woman from Detroit who'd been moved to join the protest was murdered by the Klan. It is distressing to read how the FBI campaign to smear Viola Luizza's reputation after her death wrecked the lives of her husband and five children. King was ever mindful that white allies shared the threat of retribution. President Johnson came out in favor of the Voting Rights Act and some blacks complained that he hadn't done so until whites started getting killed. The bill was signed into law on August 6, 1965, and five days later a devastating race riot broke out in the Watts section of Los Angeles, much to Johnson's confusion and hurt.

The Voting Rights Act of 1965 was the most important piece of civil rights legislation since the Fifteenth Amendment. It declared:

No voting qualifications or prerequisite to voting, or standard, practice, or procedure shall be imposed or applied by any State or political subdivision to deny or abridge the right of any citizen of the United States to vote on account of race or color.

The law abolished poll taxes, literacy tests, and other devices previously used to keep blacks from voting, such as the Chinese box, a puzzle that was impossible for anyone to solve. The Voting Rights Act recognized the assertion of federal power to regulate voting over that of the states. The law originally applied to seven southern states and allowed a federal court to appoint federal examiners to guarantee enforcement of the Fifteenth Amendment.

The most controversial provision of the Voting Rights Act obliged states to obtain "preclearance" from either the Justice Department or the US District Court for the District of Columbia before they could make changes to their electoral laws or practices, whether it be altering the shape of a voting district or designing a new ballot. In other words, the federal government had a way of finding out what the backroom boys were getting up to and anybody could act as a whistle-blower. States' rights advocates immediately challenged the legislation on those grounds, but in *South Carolina* v. *Katzenbach* (1966), the US Supreme Court—the Warren Court— upheld the law as constitutional.

The Southern Regional Council's privately funded

Voter Education Project (VEP), with Vernon Jordan at its head, sought to increase black participation in local elections throughout the South following passage of the Voting Rights Act. In 1966, the VEP financed thirty NAACP voter registration drives. Jordan said that enrollment of black voters was not enough, because black people had been alienated from the political process for too long. They had to learn what local government was and how it operated. Although the Johnson administration declined to send federal protection for registrars and voters, the number of blacks registered to vote in 1966 in Mississippi had gone up from 6 percent of those eligible to 61 percent.

Former congressman and UN ambassador Andrew Young remembers in his memoir, *An Easy Burden: The Civil Rights Movement and the Transformation of America* (1996), that the provisions for enforcement of the Voting Rights Act were so weak he wondered if Johnson hadn't stopped the southern filibuster against it in Congress by promising federal restraint. White officials in the South continued to change polling places without notice, disqualify blacks running for office on spurious grounds, or randomly purge blacks from the rolls. Young stresses that over the years, local black leaders and private citizens, through the filing of lawsuits, bore the responsibility for implementation of the legislation, including alerting the Justice Department to monitor the redrawing of congressional and state legislative districts. It was the kind of responsibility that changed the way black people felt about themselves, because they were successfully taking on the system. Young writes:

> To really change the South it was necessary for Colored signs to come down, but it was also necessary to elect men and women of goodwill to public office. Justice had to be institutionalized into the body politic and not experienced just as a response to the massive pressure of demonstration and boycotts. As we had learned from our study of the first Reconstruction, without real political power, the changes achieved with demonstrations could well be eroded over time. Blacks could not protect their newly won rights unless they shared in the decision-making process of the political system.

Stokely Carmichael, who became the new chairman of the SNCC in 1966, conceived Black Power as a repudiation of nonviolence, but in the South it also meant black communities asserting themselves through the ballot. "We're going to take over and get black sheriffs and black tax assessors," Carmichael said. But an NAACP member in charge of a registration drive in

Hattiesburg, Mississippi, was killed when his home was bombed. Away from the large towns and main roads, fear still ruled in the South.

"It was exceptionally difficult at first to get black people to go to the courthouse to register—the first step," Carmichael said in *Black Power* (1967), his manifesto calling for blacks to fashion themselves into a political force independent of conventional parties.

> The fight at that point was waged simply in terms of being able to establish within the black community a sense of the right to fight racial oppression and exploitation.... In addition, they felt that their fight would be meaningless. They remembered those who had been cut down.

James Meredith, the first black graduate of the University of Mississippi—dozens of US troops were injured by white rioters protesting his presence at the school— was shot and wounded when marching from Memphis, Tennessee, to Jackson, Mississippi, in 1966 in a personal attempt to encourage blacks in the South to register.

In the North, where the vote was thought not to have done much for black people, the call for blacks to seize power did not invoke the ballot. King endorsed Black Power as electoral influence but pleaded with

Carmichael to abandon the slogan as inflammatory. However, as the white backlash against black voter registration gained ground, Carmichael seemed to young militants to have a more realistic assessment of the political situation than King. If Black Consciousness signaled the creation of a supposedly new black value system to the young men of the SNCC who followed Carmichael from his Selma jail, then Black Power was their sudden battle cry against the old machinery of white political terror. Black Power meant control, Carmichael said in an essay in *The New York Review of Books*, published in 1966.[2]

In my memory, I am passing through the living room and catching a black-and-white glimpse, a TV picture of a black teen hurled backward by a water cannon. I don't know if I saw at the time news footage of police dogs tearing at the shirttails of demonstrators or if a documentary has since given me the image as the stand-in for what I could have seen. In the southern tradition, there was much my parents didn't want us to know.

I thought my father had gone downtown to hear Robert Kennedy address an angry black crowd after King was assassinated, but he told me the night Obama was elected that, no, that night in 1968 he'd sat in Red's

Tavern on Indiana Avenue, the preferred hangout of his crowd, too disgusted to say much. My mother had not heard that black students were staying home from school. No black classmates called me to fill me in. I was the only black kid to show up. But I was most certainly not white. My white friends could hitchhike, my parents insisted when I got to high school, but I would end up dead if I tried it.

My older sister brought home the smiling white hippie whose bare feet under the Thanksgiving table amazed my mother. My other sister introduced her Afro and a sullen Black Power advocate whose black leather jacket told my father he was a hoodlum. I was reading Antonia Fraser. My parents and their friends went into a panic as they lost control of their children in a time of serious racial strife, and they were sure that their suburban children did not know what that meant. Perfectly nice girls were dropping out of college to have babies for the revolution.

Meanwhile, the sons of the poor back in town, the inner city, were coming home dead from Vietnam. Defense Secretary Robert McNamara had said that the War on Poverty would be won if 30,000 black men joined the army. One woman we knew refused the flag offered her at her son's graveside. King had come out against the Vietnam War a year before his assassination.

Roy Wilkins, the executive director of the NAACP, said in his autobiography, *Standing Fast* (1982), that he believed at the time that King had taken a position that was contrary to the long-term interests of black people. For many of my father's World War II generation, the military had been liberation from the South, a chance to go to a white graduate school on the GI Bill, and a trouble-free opportunity to vote, by absentee ballot.

The generational divide was profound and increasingly expressed not as nonviolence versus violence, or even as integration versus black separatism, but as working within the system versus tearing it down. My father said after a visit with his Morehouse classmate, Floyd McKissick, that he'd wanted to tell him to act his age. In 1966, McKissick had succeeded James Farmer as the head of CORE, but was resigning to found in North Carolina what he called the Republic of New Africa. McKissick endorsed Nixon in the 1972 election, in return for which he received federal aid for his utopian project that became known as Soul City, which was mostly black, though open to all.

But the 1970s—that time was also the era of the "New Black Politics," as realized in the election of the twelve House members of the newly formed Congressional Black Caucus as well as that of 1,860 state and local black officials nationwide. In 1966, Edward

Brooke became the first black elected to the Senate since Reconstruction. He was a moderate Republican and the black population of Massachusetts was less than 7 percent. In his memoir, *Bridging the Divide* (2007), Brooke says that he decided that the Vietnam War, which he opposed escalating, not race, was the important issue of the campaign. He recalls that the day he was sworn in, embattled Harlem Congressman Adam Clayton Powell Jr. left office, making a dramatic exit down the Capitol steps. Brooke told Gwen Ifill that he'd received a book from President Obama inscribed, "Thank you for paving the way." Brooke was often at odds with the Congressional Black Caucus members in the House.

In the 1970s, the majority of the nation's black population was concentrated in just fifteen cities, some the decayed northern cities crippled by dwindling tax bases where black candidates were winning mayoral elections. Young Turks such as Detroit's John Conyers or Harlem's Charles Rangel compared themselves to the old guard, such as Philadelphia's then eight-term representative, Robert N. C. Nix, and declared that the days of the black ward politician loyal to the white machine were numbered.

The new generation, the Vietnam generation, found its sharpest political expression in the National Black Political Convention held in Gary, Indiana, in 1972. At the convention, organized by Gary's mayor, Richard Hatcher, and Amiri Baraka, among others, eight thousand delegates, from several political affiliations, and a number of elected black officials from across the country began to formulate how Black Power could be put to work in the electoral process. However, whites were excluded from the meeting. The Black Power agenda called for proportional representation for blacks in Congress, the end of capital punishment, the establishment of national health care, solidarity with the Palestinians, and the use of busing as a means of desegregation.

"We come to Gary in an hour of great crisis and tremendous promise for Black America," the convention's Black Agenda declared.

Our cities are crime-haunted dying grounds. Huge sectors of our youth—and countless others—face permanent unemployment. Those of us who work find our paychecks able to purchase less and less. Neither the courts nor the prisons contribute to anything resembling justice or reformation. The schools are unable—or unwilling—to educate our children for the real world of our struggles. Meanwhile, the officially approved epidemic of drugs threatens to wipe out the minds and strengths of our best young warriors.

The convention's agenda asserted that both parties betrayed black people whenever their interests conflicted with those of black people. White liberalism had failed to save black people. The convention called on black people to join the struggle to build a new society. Mayor Hatcher declared that black people were through with trusting the two major political parties. In the future, black people would rely on the power of black unity.

Supreme Court Justice Thurgood Marshall, then assistant first counsel for the NAACP's Legal Defense Fund that argued *Smith* v. *Allwright* back in 1944, reflected in an interview in 1977 that he was sure that when the decision, which eliminated all-white primaries, was handed down, "every Negro in Texas was thinking in one mind, as solid a bloc as you could find." They raised a great deal of money, but by the time of the primary two months later, "those Negroes had divided into three blocs. So where do you get your Negro bloc voting? There is no such thing. It is a myth."

After Watergate and the defeat in Vietnam, the New Left pondered why the antiwar movement had not found permanent political expression. Yet blacks experienced the administration of Jimmy Carter as the Second

Reconstruction. It was his use of federal power in the interest of black advancement that Ronald Reagan believed he'd been given a mandate to reverse. Jesse Jackson's presidential campaigns of 1984 and 1988 were important as transitions between movement politics and electoral politics, because both were necessary in a time of conservative reaction.[3]

"We have yet to find an appropriate vocabulary to describe the civil rights movement," Richard H. King observes in *Civil Rights and the Idea of Freedom* (1992), his defense of the movement's influence on political ideas. King defines it as a "movement of political rejuvenation," and an attempt to change political culture:

> The civil rights movement, along with the anti–Vietnam War movement and the emerging women's movement, forced the nation to confront more than the gap between its professed ideals and the realities of the Jim Crow South. It also triggered a rethinking on the academic and popular level of what those ideals meant in themselves. It is no coincidence that since the 1960s there has been a revival of political and social theory in America.

Yet King expresses concern that the legacy of civil rights will not endure, because what it changed has not been sufficiently taken in by political institutions and political culture in the country.

Crucial though the black vote may have been to the success of Bill Clinton's presidential campaigns, some analysts at the time were pessimistic in their assessment of the Democrats' future, because polls showed that to the average white voter the party was too identified with the social liberalism of black causes. But the future turned out to be with Ronald W. Walters when he said in *Black Presidential Politics in America* (1988) that he was confident that as a consequence of black voters having been mobilized by the Jackson campaigns, they would develop as a bloc that could make or break presidential elections. Walters envisioned blacks holding the balance of power and practicing "leverage politics" on a national scale.

After the Fairmont Conference in 1980, right-wing think tanks supported the careers of black academics who questioned the liberal assumptions of the civil rights era. Though the chances for leverage politics seemed to have receded, black politicians won office in the wilderness of the Reagan-Bush years. Douglas Wilder was governor of Virginia from 1990 to 1994, the first black governor of a state since Reconstruction. A number of black officials were elected on state and local levels, but all the attention went to the conservative attack. Maybe the conservative critique forced some black politicians to claim race neutrality, to campaign as color-blind politicians. But the change that Obama represents—the black candidate who appeals to white voters—is not sudden and he is not an isolated figure. In recent times, Deval Patrick, who became governor of Massachusetts in 2007, without having held any office previously, has had a career something like Obama's.

2.

What surprised some black Americans was that Obama didn't win by a greater margin in 2008 than he did. It took a near meltdown to put a black man in office, some said. In Kenya, they paved the road to his grandmother's house. "His election has raised an improbable hope not just for North Americans, but for the blacks of the planet, no matter their race," Édouard Glissant and Patrick Chamoiseau proclaimed in their ecstatic essay "The Intractable Beauty of the World." Obama seemed somewhat embarrassed by the Nobel Peace Prize, but that he was given the award was perhaps the Nobel Committee's way of reiterating how relieved the world was that Bush and his cronies were gone.

Historians of the civil rights movement note how young many of the participants were. When Obama first took office as a youthful president, he was eight years older than King was when he died. From the first campaign—Obama and the Clintons in Selma; Obama accepting the nomination on the anniversary of the March on Washington. The symbolism tells us that the civil rights movement is the 1960s generation's heroic struggle, its substitute war of liberation, not the Vietnam War and not the antiwar movement, either. People respond to Obama's sense of history: how much his 2004 convention speech echoed Barbara Jordan's of 1976, for instance. During the first campaign, Obama showed humility as a movement legatee and he invited the nation as a whole to share in the inheritance. He was early-1960s interracial cool's rebuke to late-1960s militant separatism.

A black man was in the White House while conditions for the majority of black people compared to those of white people as measured by employment, income, education, housing, and high infant mortality rates were as poor as they had been in 1960. But black people weren't expecting the first black president to do anything for them as black people. His sheer being there had done so much. They, like millions of others, were looking for relief as citizens in a troubled economy.

A different understanding of American history may explain why for some people, especially black people, race was a major issue in the 2008 campaign after all. It was hard to credit when a white person said that he or she did not see Obama as a black man. They meant that he did not fit their idea of what a black man was, which was too brutal an admission. The question of what a black man was supposed to be and who was asking explained the reservations the old guard in black politics had when it contemplated the next generation.

Jesse Jackson criticized Obama in 2007 when he stayed away from a march in Jena, Louisiana, protesting the imprisonment of six black teenagers on false charges. What was the point of electing blacks to high office if they gave up their ties to the black community, some asked. Moses laid hands on Joshua so that his people could avenge themselves on their enemies. But black America had changed, psychologically, because it had changed large sectors of white America.

My mother did not hesitate in her support of Obama. She who never had an interest in sports simply moved her enthusiasm for Tiger Woods over to Obama. But my

father stood by the Clintons, even through furious battles with my sisters over three-strikes laws and the cen-
trist policies of the Democratic Leadership Council. I
remember that when my mother was refusing to have
her cataracts removed, my father read to her. Not po-
etry or Thackeray, her favorite, but Bill Clinton's autobiography. He read aloud every word of *My Life*. They
had such a good time that even after she finally had the
procedure he still read to her, going through Hillary
Clinton's memoir, *Living History*. Comforter, I am thy
comforter. They did not get around to *Dreams from My
Father*.

My father could perhaps understand the complexity
of Jesse Jackson's tears the night he watched Obama in
victory in Grant Park in Chicago. My father's embarrassed ambivalence about our first black president was
an expression of his anxiety that he and his generation
were being pushed aside, that Obama's optimism about
the country's long-term future meant that the truth of
his generation's experience in a segregated America
could be forgotten. And perhaps he was being visited by
an old person's jealousy of a younger person who has so
much open road ahead of him still.

But my father would have recognized the white
people of the Tea Party and in some ways been reassured. Tea Party people seemed to me much like the

white people in the 1950s who were furious with *Brown v. Board of Education*, white people determined to obstruct implementation of desegregation orders. *All Deliberate Speed* (2004) by Charles J. Ogletree Jr. made the case that resistance to desegregation was not confined to mobs. Local and state officials, as well as some in the executive branch, also joined the defiance of court orders. When I was tempted to dismiss as the last gasp of a dying order the white people who screamed that because of Obama's policies socialism was being imposed on them, I recalled that those angry officials and citizens' councils in the 1950s succeeded in stopping meaningful school and neighborhood integration in many parts of the South not just for a long while but for good.[4]

The conspiratorial state attorneys general who resented *Brown v. Board of Education*, the recalcitrant federal judges, the apoplectic parents who loathed the Warren Court and loved the rhetoric of states' rights can be linked to the Secessionist mood that lingered in the South. One version of our political legacy from Reconstruction says that the federal authorities enforce unpopular but remedial laws on race while the states— i.e., the South—fight to keep the status quo. Another version of this legacy says that the rights of the states shield Americans from the tyrannies of centralization. Perhaps they are in essence two different notions of constitutional guarantee, a matter of which political entity best protects the individual: the federal government or state governments. Traditionally, blacks have had only federal power to rely on. The majority of black people would perhaps argue that the Fourteenth Amendment was framed so that the Bill of Rights could be applied to the individual states.

My father objected to *Mississippi Burning*, the film about the murder of the three civil rights workers in the state in 1964. The film credited the FBI with bringing the murderers to justice. The truth was that the FBI had to be harassed into sending agents down to investigate and when they got there everybody knew who the murderers were.[5] *Mississippi Burning* made the villains out to be freaks, extremists, not like us. Historically, American film and literature have tended to portray racists as lower-class. "Atticus is a gentleman!" Jim shouts happily about his father in *To Kill a Mockingbird*. People are assured that they're not racist because they're not "like that." These days it is easier to insult someone's class than his race. Someone who makes $200,000 a year will say he is middle-class and yet so will someone who makes $40,000.

President Carter was right when he said that racism was behind much of the hostility to President Obama. But I also see why Obama couldn't agree with Carter.

The dignity of the executive office was at stake. When Obama booked himself on Sunday morning talk shows to talk about health care reform, not race, that in itself was a lesson in race politics. We saw, when David Paterson claimed that there was a racist conspiracy to keep him from running for the governor's office in New York, how out of control it made him seem. It sounded as though he couldn't handle the pressures of dirty politics. Even if true, the accusation gave a bad impression, like a poor alibi. Our commander in chief cannot allow himself to come across as a victim. The world is listening.

Anthony Painter in *Barack Obama: The Movement for Change* (2009), written in the glow of Obama's first victory, sees his election in 2008 as a culmination of the dream of black-white-brown political action that Martin Luther King and Jesse Jackson brought to Chicago and that Harold Washington revived in 1983 as his winning strategy in the contest to be the city's mayor. Painter interprets American politics as a succession of coalitions, with the New Deal coalition collapsing in the social turmoil of 1968 and the juggernaut of organized populist conservatism emerging from the backlash.

In 2008, it was the turn of the conservative coalition

to fall apart. "One of the tests of his presidency will be his ability to morph Obama '08 into a self-sustaining movement for change based upon a new civic activism," Painter says. "Where the right-wing conservative movement seized upon fear and division, Obama has the opportunity to create a political force based on justice that will go beyond his own period of office in the White House." The 2008 election had been about race, while the 2012 election, though a referendum on Obama's administration, was more about the new grassroots force in electoral politics, the Chicago coalition, coming into its own, proving itself.

Obama's reelection stimulated concern in some quarters about the price black Americans were paying for a black president. Fredrick C. Harris, a professor of political science at Columbia University, charged in a *New York Times* opinion piece just prior to the 2012 election that black elites were failing in their duty to challenge racial inequality. The prophetic tradition among black intellectuals of speaking truth to power had become enfeebled. Blacks debated social policy under Clinton while supporting Clinton, but they had fallen silent under Obama.

Black poverty stood at 28 percent, compared to 10 percent for whites; black unemployment was 13 percent compared to 7 percent for whites. Yet Obama had little to say about race and poverty, although his expansion of national health care was the most significant social legislation since the Great Society, as Harris noted. Harris also criticized Obama's administration for doing little in the way of criminal justice reform. He claimed that what he viewed as Obama's race-neutral governing style was a false kind of universalism. Harris said he wasn't asking what a black president was doing for blacks but rather how was a Democratic president helping his most loyal constituency.

In *The Price of the Ticket: Barack Obama and the Rise and Decline of Black Politics* (2012), Harris goes on to argue that Malcolm X's and Stokely Carmichael's vision of independent black politics had lost out to activist Bayard Rustin's idea of coalition politics. Rustin believed that the separatist tendencies within the movement ought to be resisted and that blacks had to build alliances within the Democratic Party. In writing about the situation in Mississippi for *Commentary* in 1965, Rustin observed:

A conscious bid for political power is being made, and in the course of that effort a tactical shift is being effected: direct-action techniques are being subordinated to a strategy calling for the building of community institutions and power bases.

Clearly, the implications of the shift reach far beyond Mississippi. What began as a protest movement is being challenged to translate itself into a political movement.

Rustin saw black voters not as a swing bloc but as part of a progressive partnership with trade unionists, religious groups, intellectuals.

It would seem from Harris's own account that Rustin's coalition, his issue-based alliances, put Jesse Jackson within striking distance of the Democratic nomination in 1988 in a way that Jackson's boldness as the candidate of black discontent had not in 1984. Because of Jackson's strength, blacks gained places in the Democratic Party leadership and changes in primary rules that would ultimately benefit Obama's candidacy. Yet it was the sort of black activism Stokely Carmichael advocated that allowed Harold Washington to upset the Chicago Democratic Party machine and become the city's first black mayor in 1983. Solid black and Latino support won him reelection in 1987. Though remembered as a coalition builder, Harris points out, Washington, who died six months into his second term, had received only 20 percent of the white vote. It was not coalition politics but rather, as Harris calls it, a simple formula:

One viable black candidate running with solid black support against multiple white candidates splitting the white vote had a more than even chance of winning in a citywide, statewide, or countrywide contest.

Carol Moseley Braun's successful Senate bid in Illinois in 1992 was the breakthrough race, preparing the way for Obama. The white people Braun appealed to were women.

Obama's first congressional bid in Chicago in 2000 reflected the ideological divide between those committed to an independent black politics and those who believed in empowerment through coalitions. Obama lost and went back to the Illinois state legislature, where he fashioned a reputation for being able to get bills through with bipartisan support, much of it legislation important to blacks. He won even in conservative downstate Illinois in his race for the Senate in 2007. But, Harris contends, as his electoral prospects widened, Obama spoke out less on special issues affecting blacks. Indeed, in Harris's view, Obama as a presidential candidate went from being an advocate for the black poor to being a critic of the behavior of the black poor. The "politics of respectability" demanded that he blame the black poor, as did conservatives, for their problems, as a way of controlling them. Harris says that blacks were as receptive to Obama's message as whites were reassured. Obama's recovery program in 2009 had no jobs bill or specific remedies for minorities, Harris observes:

> Malcom X's vision of black politics, centered on putting community issues first, has collapsed under the weight of the Democratic Party's general uneasiness about tackling racial inequality and under the guidance of a race-neutral black president who distances himself from issues and policies targeted at eradicating racial inequality.

Obama's universalism had "morphed" into a race-neutral or color-blind approach to policy that sidelined issues important to black voters, who accepted the situation because they felt that Obama had to be protected from the right. His presidency matters as symbolic representation, but his administration has not been able to bring about substantial change for those who most need it, Harris concludes.

There was a time—1865—when most everything about the way American society worked had to be explained to the mass of black people, because as an enslaved people they had been kept in such a benighted condition, the feeling went. Schoolmarms and pastors from the North, white and black alike, regarded the en-culturation of former slaves as their mission. W.E.B. Du Bois at the turn of the twentieth century said that black people faced an appalling work of social reform, that regardless of how barbarously blacks had been treated in the past they nevertheless had to make every sacrifice in order to become fit members of the community as quickly as possible. Modern society had too many other problems for blacks to be burdens, he added.

Far into the twentieth century, the sociology of our behavior was an important aspect of discussion about what were considered inner-city problems. In general, where liberals, both black and white, saw symptoms of deep social disorders, conservatives, both black and white, saw types of behavior as the causes of social turmoil. Some black voters were happy to support Jesse Jackson and said that he was a role model for black youth. It had to do with the self-consciousness of repre-sentation, of being always an ambassador of the race, a circumstance that, to judge from the number of mem-oirs on the subject, produced a peculiar anxiety in black students who found themselves among upper-class white students at elite schools in the 1980s and 1990s.

However, judgment of how blacks behave still has more to do with the self-consciousness of integration, of having to prove ourselves worthy of inclusion. To many blacks, exhortations about or reproaches for our behavior can come across as a way of saying that blacks are not ready to participate fully in American society. Any black barbershop audience will tell you that no other group in the US is spoken to or about in this language, only the people who are not the descendants of immigrants. But they will add without hesitation that some black people need to hear such reprimands for not living up to their responsibilities.

In 2004, Bill Cosby made a notable speech in which he called on blacks to be better parents. Cosby's work in education made his an authoritative voice. Moreover, throughout the Reagan years, *The Cosby Show*, his socially aware, relaxed comedy about a middle-class black family, was the number-one television show in the US. But the suicide attacks and massacres and beheadings in Iraq in 2004 had a subtle effect on the nation's morale and the view of how much a citizen's right to vote should depend on his or her being a nice guy. The American occupation of Iraq made the controversy about black behavior seem rather backward, a debate that felt like a throwback to the days of arguing about whether certain social pathologies should be seen as consequences of racism.

We mostly associate critiques of black behavior with the strategies of neoconservative black academics and commentators. They countered the argument for government engagement in social engineering by promoting a social view that held that the obstacles to taking advantage of the opportunities that existed in our open society had to do with an individual black person's character. However, when Obama in 2008 told MTV that the brothers should pull up their pants, he sounded like a black man who was keeping it real. Harris and other critics of Obama's relationship to his black supporters forget the political significance of Obama's quiet speech about race in Philadelphia during the 2008 campaign.

The sheer presence of the Obamas has made it harder to introduce "race" as a tactic to scare and unify the white vote. The president is not to blame that the Trayvon Martin case in Florida in 2012 seemed to say that not much had changed, after all. Stand-your-ground and no-duty-to-retreat laws were really just whites-can-still-shoot-blacks-with-impunity laws, some charged. The disapproval among some white people that Obama had expressed sympathy for the murdered black teenager was an added bitterness. But Obama as a symbol will remain powerful past his tenure. The credit denied him now accrues anyway. He is a large part of the reason that the majority of white youth regard Tea Party–style white nationalism with such disdain.[6]

We complained all that summer of the 2012 campaign about the amount of e-mail, but the electronic barrage turned out to have been a manifestation of a sophisticated, secretly confident campaign. The advantage that the Republican Party had when awash with the mailing lists of the Christian Right all those Lee Atwater and Karl Rove years ago had gone with the changes in the technology of mass communication. As a consequence, Obama's campaign had something of the insurgent atmosphere of going over the heads of politicians to speak directly to the people. Obama surprised a number of people during the 2012 campaign when he logged on to the entertainment, news, and social-networking website Reddit.

The 2012 election told us that the Solid South of the Republicans was weakening because of the changed demographics of the region, including the fact that black people have been moving back down to the Old Country for the first time since World War II. They are leaving northern cities and towns. The West is speaking Spanish; openly gay men and lesbians are being counted as 5 percent of the electorate. Blacks outvoted whites. In response, the right wing has reverted to the customs of voter suppression and attempts to redraw districts, and succeeded in passing legislation that made photo IDs mandatory for voting in many states.

At the time of the 2012 presidential election, thirty-one states had some kind of photo ID requirement for voters; seven had less strict laws; five states had such laws under judicial review; and four had tough measures in place. It was not easy for some segments of the population to get the ID, something middle-class lawmakers seemed to have a hard time believing. Photo ID requirements were not only a factor down South.

The US Supreme Court upheld Indiana's voter ID law in 2008. But when Pennsylvania's Republican legislature and governor enacted a strict new photo ID law in 2012, a judge granted a temporary injunction against its implementation on the grounds that to try to put it into effect so soon before the election would most likely result in the disqualification of eligible voters. A federal court in Texas struck down its voter ID law in the summer of 2012 because it would impose "unforgiving burdens on the poor." Republicans in Wisconsin lamented that if it had had a voter ID law, Romney would have won the state.

Word leaked out of Florida that the Republicans tried to stop early voting, because the indications were that it was going in Obama's favor. Ta-Nehisi Coates maintained in his blog for *The Atlantic Monthly* shortly after the 2012 election that voter suppression backfired in

Ohio, that trying to confine early voting to weekdays only made people more determined to cast their votes. What is good for minorities is good for the nation as a whole. The civil rights movement had given the US a way to escape McCarthyism. Now the civil rights movement must become a human rights movement. It is altogether striking that on election day Twitter kept up morale among people who resolved not to be moved, no matter the length of the line or the hour. In a story on Obama's techno power, *US News & World Report* listed Flickr, Digg, LinkedIn, and Myspace among several websites that figured in his having had so much more influence in social media than his opponent.

In *The Audacity of Hope*, the traditions of Congress and how it is supposed to legislate matter to Obama. He almost sounds like a good old boy thrilled to walk the corridors of power. Then came legislative battles as seen from the Oval Office—and Obama deployed Twitter. Similar instant-message pressure from constituents influenced the congressional vote on health care, raising the possibility that the digital age could bring the direct democracy that the Founding Fathers mistrusted, which is why we have the strangeness of the Electoral College to begin with.

We had been waiting since 1972 for the youth vote—white youth—to show up. Facebook told us that the young—white kids—finally had and that social media such as Facebook probably did as much if not more to get out this vote than knocking on doors did. Facebook was studying the effects of its campaign applications and found that it may have delivered as many as 320,000 new young voters to the polls in 2012. It predicted that because of its apps, these young voters would become habitual voters sympathetic to the Democratic Party. The friend list seemed beyond Republican reach. The White House's and Obama's Facebook and Twitter accounts are among the most followed in the world.

In a documentary made in 1963, James Baldwin can be seen talking to unemployed black youth in San Francisco. In answer to their hopelessness, he insists that they can be anything they set their minds to. "There will be a Negro president of this country, but it will not be the country we are sitting in now," Baldwin assures them. He was right. "Dear White America, You are not alone. Yours sincerely, the Dreadful Sundry of the World." A week after the 2012 election, *The New York Times* published graphs charting the blocs of voters Obama had won—women, the under-thirties, blacks, Asians, Hispanics, gay people, the unmarried, working mothers of young children, people with graduate degrees, people without high school diplomas, Jews, Catholics, people in big cities, and poor people.

Social questions do not advance uniformly. For instance, few heroes of the civil rights era had sexual politics that today would be considered progressive. In 1964, Stokely Carmichael made his infamous remark that the only position of women in the SNCC was "prone" and we're not surprised by his black macho, even if his defenders say that that was not the real Stokely. However, we are surprised that it was Bayard Rustin who blocked having a woman speaker at the March on Washington in 1963. According to Dorothy Height's memoir, *Open Wide the Freedom Gates* (2003), Rustin argued that black women would be represented because they were already active in the organizations sponsoring the march. We might think that because Rustin was gay and other civil rights figures conspired to sideline him, he should have had Baldwin's sensitivity to black women's history.

After the 2012 election, I thought that Republicans would hurl themselves onto the Latino vote, like seals slamming into a bright big school of fish, especially in Texas, which is 38 percent Hispanic and where one in five Hispanics in America lives. But in 2012 the Hispanic vote was 48 percent of those eligible, down from 49.9 percent in 2008.[7] More Hispanics are registered as Democrats than as Republicans. Yet these days the newspapers report Latino disillusionment with the electoral process. This detachment may be related to how unwelcome white-controlled institutions can make a Latino person feel. A friend of mine who teaches primary school in Los Angeles County was stunned when the school's principal told her that the salaries of the special tutors she proposed for her Spanish-speaking students would come from her paycheck. It is not entirely clear that the Republicans want the Hispanic vote to increase, though immigration is maybe an issue they could get their right wing to compromise on.

However, women's issues are, for reasons of prejudice, past discussion for most conservatives. Women were more of a voting bloc in 2012. Women were openly voting in women's interests, and therefore voting against the Republican platform. The increase in the black vote in 2012 to 66 percent of those eligible was due to a high turnout among black women. The Census Bureau tells us that there are fifty-three million unmarried women in the US. They alone comprise 25 percent of the electorate. Stop, children, what's that sound. Everybody look what's going down, I heard. I assumed it was Hillary, the forty-fifth president, coming around the mountain.

I have a few hip friends, black and white, who didn't vote in 2012. They have never voted since I've known them, citizens who say that it makes no difference which major party wins. The matter of which political party gets to appoint judges doesn't mean the same thing to them that it does to most black people. There is no such thing as not voting, David Foster Wallace said. It's the faith I grew up in. I lied to my parents in 1980 about having voted, a year when I was too out of it to walk one city block to register.

But in the faith I grew up in, a central tenet holds that American justice is on our side. Tocqueville and the Whig interpretation of history are on our side. America stands for progress, of which the expansion and defense of democracy have been a necessary part. The US has a lot to answer for, starting with the "a slave is only three-fifths of a person" formula that the Founding Fathers came up with. Some might start with the displacement or decimation of the tribal nations that were already here. But the historical truth and the Constitution will agree in the long run. It is a document with a conscience. We just have to show up every two years. This is what my father and my mother taught my sisters and me.[8]

I used to think it was funny that when my parents first voted in the suburban township where we moved in 1966, the polling station was in a country club that didn't even admit Jews. Now I see my mother make a face and dismiss the situation as nothing. I'd never thought what a humiliating experience that might have been for her, she who did not believe in black country clubs either.

3.

Obama's election should not be regarded as a culmination, Debo P. Adegbile warns in an essay included in *The Most Fundamental Right: Contrasting Perspectives on the Voting Rights Act* (2012), edited by Daniel McCool. Obama's victory should be seen as a new chapter in an evolving story.[9]

Adegbile, the associate director of the NAACP Legal Defense Fund, successfully argued before the Supreme Court in 2009 in *Northwest Austin Municipal Utility District Number One* v. *Holder* against a challenge to the federal preclearance provision of the Voting Rights Act. At that time, Section 5 called for federal court approval of changes in voting in sixteen states covered under the statute.

The enforcement provisions of the Voting Rights Act, temporary measures that had to be renewed or reauthorized by Congress periodically, were extended four times, most recently in 2006. The extension received bipartisan support in the end. While conservatives were willing to flatter the Voting Rights Act as historically important legislation, they did so in order to get rid of preclearance—that need to seek federal approval for changes in voting practices. They argued that the measure was insulting to the states under its jurisdiction because these states had changed and therefore the measure was out of date.

But Adegbile countered that jurisdictions such as Louisiana or Texas were under federal obligation precisely because in those states voting rights violations persisted. Adegbile also pointed out that because minority voting rights had been protected in Florida, Louisiana, North Carolina, South Carolina, and Georgia, these states, though covered, nevertheless elected blacks to Congress in the 1990s for the first time since Reconstruction. In 2011, discriminatory redistricting plans in Texas, Louisiana, and Alabama were halted, if only temporarily, because of Section 5. The evidence before the courts and Congress illustrated how necessary federal supervision was still. "The constitutional attacks have not succeeded since 1965," Adegbile warned, "but neither have they ceased."

I remember thinking how interested in Adegbile's essay my father would have been. I missed, at last, his tedious insistence on race, my historian of charismatic movements, my collective behavior analyst, my own personal resource mobilization theorist. During the 2012 election, I missed his voice, his incorrigibility, his bibliographical reach. Most of the books from which I got my overview of the history of the black vote came from the swayed shelves in his den. I looked back and was moved by how much he knew about the subject, how much of his mental being he'd given to the freedom struggle.

And then in June 2013 it happened: the Supreme Court struck down as unconstitutional the preclearance provision of the Voting Rights Act.

In his majority opinion—surely concurring Justice Clarence Thomas's name will live on in infamy—in *Shelby County, Alabama* v. *Holder,* Chief Justice John Roberts, though he gives the credit for increased participation of minorities in the electoral process to the Voting Rights Act, nevertheless uses the very success of the Voting Rights Act against it.

The "blight of racial discrimination in voting" hadn't been seen in the covered jurisdictions since the law was enacted. Voter turnout and registration numbers had almost reached parity and minority candidates held offices at unprecedented levels, he writes. Blatant discriminatory evasions of federal decrees were rare. Roberts takes the view that the law has done its job, that the conditions that had originally justified such measures have been eliminated, and that there is no longer any historical need for its most stringent and potent provisions. He does not agree that the robustness of the law has been a deterrent all these years, or that, once sprung from the burden of federal accountability, long-covered jurisdictions might have recourse to new means by which to achieve the old aim: voter exclusion.

The Voting Rights Act was a temporary measure, he asserts, which was why it had to be renewed periodically by Congress. The coverage formula determined in Section 4(b) of the law and the restrictions called for in Section 5 had been reauthorized over the years as though nothing had changed in the covered states. "In fact, the Act's unusual remedies have grown even stronger." He claims that to accept Section 5 as a deterrent only places that section of the law beyond effective scrutiny.

Current burdens have to be justified by current needs and he finds that the coverage formula of 1965 no longer meets that need. Coverage was being determined by what Roberts calls "decades-old data and eradicated practices." Racial disparity no longer existed in the numbers that fifty years ago justified the preclearance remedy or the coverage formula—meaning that districts to be covered were those that had a history of recent voting tests, low voter registration, and low voter turnout. The government, he argues, can no longer establish the relevance of the solution to the problem. The extraordinary conditions that obtained in 1965 were the reason the Supreme Court of the time upheld legislation "otherwise unfamiliar to our federal system."

His most galling language has to do with states' rights. Because the Constitution leaves to individual states most of the decisions about the machinery of how elections are conducted, he judges Section 5 of the Voting Rights Act to be "a drastic departure from basic principles of federalism" and "an equally dramatic departure from the principle that all States enjoy equal sovereignty." Some uncovered states recently had a worse record of discrimination than covered states. Counties in New Hampshire, New York, and California have at one time been covered jurisdictions. The Fifteenth Amendment was not designed to punish for the past, he says.

In her dissent, Justice Ruth Bader Ginsburg reproaches the Court for in effect usurping Congress's obligation to enforce post–Civil War amendments by appropriate legislation. The principle of equal sovereignty of the states did not apply, in that it had to do with the readmission of states to the Union, and there were a number of instances in which states were treated differently.

The Voting Rights Act was the instrument by which the country's strides in voter equality had been taken, yet the Court was terminating the remedy that had been shown to be the best weapon against discrimination in voting. Historically, whenever one form of voting discrimination was prohibited, she notes, other means were found to disenfranchise minorities. Over the years, the Court has encountered a variety of laws designed to suppress the minority vote. In the past, it recognized that discrimination against minority voters was a political problem that required a political solution.

Circumstances reduce what Ginsburg calls "the ameliorative potential of legislative Acts" intended to control electoral practices, and slow, difficult case-by-case litigation is also inadequate, given the scale of the problem. Consequently, the Voting Rights Act was, to her mind, one of the most "amply justified exercises of federal legislative power in our Nation's history." The most important point is that voter discrimination still exists; it has not been eradicated. Justice Ginsburg sees a need for preclearance when it comes to "second-generation barriers" to minority voting.

Where denying minorities access to registration or the polls has been a form of discrimination associated with the past, the new form of discrimination is in the direction of trying to reduce the impact of the minority vote by gerrymandering, redrawing districts, or at-large voting instead of district-by-district voting. A city could annex white suburbs to dilute the black vote within the old city limits, for instance. "Whatever the device employed, this Court has long recognized that vote dilution, when adopted with a discriminatory purpose, cuts down the right to vote as certainly as denial of access to the ballot."

Ginsburg disposes of Roberts's contentions about states' rights by simply pointing out that Congress has the power to act decisively when defending the most fundamental right in our democratic system and that deference to this authority is well grounded in the Constitution and by precedent. She reminds us of Chief Justice John Marshall's opinion in 1819 in *McCulloch v. Maryland*:

> Let the end be legitimate, let it be within the scope of the constitution, and all means which are appropriate, which are plainly adapted to that end, which are not prohibited, but consist with the letter and spirit of the constitution, are constitutional.

Justice Ginsburg on the Fourteenth and Fifteenth Amendments:

> The stated purpose of the Civil War Amendments was to arm Congress with the power and authority to protect all persons within the Nation from violations of their rights by the States.

In 2006, she goes on to say, the reauthorization of the Voting Rights Act for twenty-five years—passed in the Senate by 98 to 0—fully satisfied the standard of review as defined by Marshall. Congress is entitled to consider preexisting records in its deliberation. She rejects Roberts's opinion that the coverage formula is "irrational" in the present age and offers several examples of continued constitutional violations. She looks closely at the record in Shelby County, Alabama, itself and is eloquent about why the Court has remained silent on why Shelby County could mount a facial challenge to the legislation in the first place.

Ginsburg states that it is not the responsibility of the Court to substitute its judgment for that of Congress when Congress has reviewed sufficient evidence to conclude that racial discrimination in voting in the covered districts remains "serious and pervasive." Ginsburg also refutes the majority opinion that the Voting Rights Act is "static, unchanged since 1965." It was designed to be "a dynamic statute, capable of adjusting to changing conditions." She finds that second-generation barriers have emerged as substitutes for first-generation barriers and that the Court has erred "egregiously" in overriding Congress.

As David Cole observes in his reflections on *Shelby County* v. *Holder*, the Supreme Court's five conservative justices forgot their own conservative tenet not to invalidate the legislation of an elected body of the people unless it clearly violated the written Constitution. The civil rights statute offended their view that the law ought to be color-blind. It is clear to Cole that the justices were prepared to abandon all judicial restraint in the case. "They object to laws that take race into account, even for purposes of protecting minorities against discrimination."

We have, in Cole's words, a radical Court, not a conservative one, an activist Court willing to hinder the federal government's ability to enforce the Fourteenth and Fifteenth Amendments by either ignoring or repudiating decades of precedent set by that very court. "A majority of the Court believes that the time for legal measures designed to redress the nation's long history of subordinating black citizens is past, and that the way forward is through mandated color-blindness." In its decisions on voting rights and affirmative action, Cole says, the Court has in effect turned the Equal Protection Clause on its head, making white plaintiffs and states the beneficiaries.[10]

Hours after the Supreme Court decision, the Texas attorney general announced that its voter ID law, which had been blocked under the Voting Rights Act, was back in effect. Texas Governor Rick Perry claimed that it was necessary in order to combat voter fraud. But MSNBC correspondent Zachary Roth found that the governor's claims were entirely unsupported by the evidence and that in his thirteen years in office, the governor could cite only two fraudulent votes out of more than eighteen million votes cast that might have been stopped or detected by voter IDs.

In 2013, the Supreme Court struck down proof of citizenship such as a birth certificate or a passport as a requirement for registering to vote in federal elections. However, Justice Antonin Scalia allowed that authorities could ask for such proofs of citizenship in state or local elections. In March 2014, a federal judge ruled that the Election Assistance Commission, a federal body, had to add instructions for Arizona and Kansas that people registering to vote in state and local elections would have to produce evidence of citizenship. Critics charged that the ruling would create a two-tier system of registration.

Section 2 of the Voting Rights Act prohibits racial discrimination in voting and, as Roth reported, the provision will be a considerable factor in challenges to voter ID laws. It forbids not only voting laws that have the intention to discriminate but also those that discriminate in effect. Conservatives want to limit Section 2 to cases where a deliberate intent to discriminate can be proven. Because of a memo against a broad interpretation of Section 2 that Justice Roberts wrote while at the Justice Department during the Reagan administration, it is thought that he is among those who want to curtail Section 2.

Since the Supreme Court decision in *Shelby County v. Holder,* Republican-controlled legislatures have ended same-day registration in Ohio and weekend voting in Wisconsin. North Carolina's Republicans in 2013 passed what *The New York Times* called the nation's most restrictive voting laws. These measures have met resistance from groups such as Project Vote, Demos, the NAACP, and Battleground Texas. The Moral Monday protests, civil disobedience in state legislatures that began in North Carolina in 2013 and then sprang up in South Carolina and Georgia, suggest that some political will exists at the grassroots level. And it is gratifying that Rush Limbaugh freaked out when he heard that California planned to mail voter registration forms to four million people who had applied for coverage under the Affordable Care Act.

Resistance is out there, yet I run from *The New York Times* some mornings because of articles predicting that the Republicans will retain the House in 2014, maybe even gain control of the Senate. I don't require the optimism of the sect: fear not, we have the answers. The demographics are on our side, but it is striking how diminished the sense of victory is among Democrats since the 2012 election. To have won 70 percent of the youth vote translated into political capital that people said Obama could use for criminal justice reform. If Obama can get the US out of the wars in Afghanistan and Iraq, then he can get us out of the ill-conceived War on Drugs that has done so much to criminalize the black population, people said. It's as though the election results have been nullified by the other branches of government that are in the hands of conservatives.

Histories of voting in the US tell us that the majority of the Founding Fathers were apprehensive about what was then thought of as universal suffrage. Benjamin Franklin cautioned the Constitutional Convention that if the Republic was going to call on citizens to defend it, then these men ought to be worthy of the vote. But the poor could not necessarily be trusted to protect the rights of property, many of his fellow delegates worried, and the poor might come together as a body, vote their interests.

The Constitution originally said little about the vote as a right and spoke instead of guaranteeing to each state a republican form of government. In the US, the vote has been a much-debated and set-upon instrument, from the questions of who has authority over the vote, local, state, or federal, and who is eligible to vote (in the early expansion of U.S. territory, aliens and noncitizens were given the vote in some locations) to when and how we vote (the secret ballot was widely used by the 1850s, coinciding with the invention of the hydraulic press and the increase in literacy in the US.) As industry grew, conservatives feared a voting urban population, a proletariat roiled by grievance. The conservative argument against universal suffrage had not changed since colonial times: some people, the degraded in particular, were incapable of making sound political judgments. For conservatives, the vote was not a right but a franchise that could be extended or withdrawn depending on social conditions.

Whiteness didn't always mean freedom in eighteenth-century America, where white slaves and indentured white servants were significant in number, as Nell Irvin Painter notes in *The History of White People* (2010). However, by the mid-1850s,

> mere adult maleness had replaced eighteenth-century requirements of a stake in society (property ownership, tax paying) and political independence

(one's own steady income) before a man could vote. With the vote came inclusion in public life, so that the antebellum period associated with the rise of the Jacksonian common man witnessed the first major extension of the meaning of what it meant to be American.

Because "poor men could be welcomed into the definition of American," it also represented what Painter calls "the first enlargement of American whiteness."

The immigrants of the late nineteenth century—from the Balkans and Italy or Polish Catholics and Russian Jews—made established immigrant communities acceptable as Americans. The second great enlargement of American whiteness "came with such reluctance and with so many qualifications and insults that Irish Americans continued to feel excluded and aggrieved." Political patronage and government employment were opportunities for economic advancement, especially for the Irish, in the cities, and they battled to keep out those they considered beneath them in the social hierarchy of American life. Among the definers and defenders of Americanness, Painter cites the influence of Jefferson and Emerson and their beliefs, based on myth, that America's foundations were Anglo-Saxon.

Mexican-Americans were defined as white by the

federal government and could vote in Texas's all-white primaries in the 1930s. There were far fewer then than there are now. During World War II, they fought in white units and looked set to join Italians and Jews in the social mobility made possible by the postwar economic boom. However, blacks were locked out of the suburbs and out of Americanness itself in the war's aftermath. The third enlargement of whiteness came with a high degree of antiblack feeling as a bonding agent. Never was the popular image of the American more Norman Rockwell Teutonic.

Race is an idea, not a fact, Painter reminds us, and what it means to be white is changing in a culture that now elevates diversity as a social goal and a young mixed-race population as an aesthetic ideal. The history of the enlargement of the franchise—women, blacks, and Native Americans were included in the twentieth century—merges at last with the expanding definitions of what it means to be American.

Part of the resistance to the post-1960s federal programs was that they put whites with blacks, which made some whites feel that they had hit bottom. It has often perplexed people on the left that poor or working-class whites would rather vote against their interests than ally with or be identified with black interests. Now that times have become desperate even for the middle class, the public picture of poverty is no longer exclusively black. As Jacqueline Jones concludes in *A Dreadful Deceit: The Myth of Race from the Colonial Era to Obama's America* (2013):

> The success of the American democratic project depends upon public policies that take into account two distinct but interrelated aspects of the nation's political economy: first, the enduring institutional structures produced by narratives of race, and second, the recent economic transformations that reach deep into the lives of many Americans regardless of their skin color or heritage.

For the longest time, I believed that at heart most Americans wanted to live in an equitable society, and it was only when we were terrified for the economic future that we forgot their best selves. Everyone said that the well-off tended to go to the polls more regularly than the economically disadvantaged did. It was hard for the poor to vote. Therefore, I was convinced that the country described for us in the mainstream media was not the true nation. The real America kept some distance from the official America in order to get on with the business of living. Already 50 percent of children in the United States under the age of one belong to a minority group.

We won't have another black president anytime soon,
people say. Black people are going to catch hell once
Obama leaves office, some black people say. It's not that
our troubles have come back, they say. It's that these
troubles never went away. One thing about pessimism is
that it feels sane. Pessimists are those who can't be taken
in, people who can't be fooled. I told you so. But it is
also a habit of mind. It reconciles us to being powerless.
It justifies detachment, indifference. It is even fear of
having power, as was that old feeling among some black
people that by the time we got somewhere, that place
was no good anymore. If we're here, then wherever we
are must have declined from what it had been before us.
Maybe that feeling hasn't entirely gone away and maybe
it will finally pass with the civil rights generation.

These days America is much less like the country we
had in mind and getting more controlled, cordoned off,
prohibited, restricted, under surveillance. The young
know whom to blame. There are some white people
who would rather see the country wrecked than have
anything work under President Obama. It is a shock
that racism in US political life is so virulent that the
heirs of white supremacy, unwilling to face the proph-
ecy in the demographics, would rather destroy it all

than hand it over. It, this land, is theirs. Before World War I, America knew robber-baron rapacity and dangerous inequality, but back then the sense of the world's resources was that they'd never run out. This time, something different is out there.

Thomas Piketty's sensation, *Capital in the Twenty-First Century* (2013), is a book I would have given to my father, interested as he was in the question of how so much of the world's wealth is becoming increasingly concentrated in very few hands. I think I will get it for myself, with its intimidating graphs, in case underlying everything going on in America is a sense that times of misery are ahead, at home and abroad, and that now that we realize resources are finite, things are beginning to fall apart. The rich are raising those feudal draw-bridges again. How mean and primitive America looks and sounds close up at the moment. Meanwhile, millions of targeted dollars are pouring through our politics and into our heads. *Citizens United* v. *Federal Election Commission* may be the worst Supreme Court decision since *Plessy* v. *Ferguson*, but black people are not brought up to believe in the cyclical view of history.

Everywhere in the West, governments are undermined by or find it prudent to appease corporations that are supranational. The postwar institutions that were the means by which we belong to the world are failing.

A great secular age of democratic experiment in which our federal government had now and then discovered its place is fading. The history of black people in America is full of paradox, the latest of which is that black people and their allies are now the defenders of the nation-state, having been, traditionally, the victims and opponents of state power.

I remember that morning after the presidential election in 1972 when I consoled a friend in a downpour. The rain came down so hard it bounced up from the walks. The mist was so thick it seemed the whole campus was lost in smoke. The courtyard of our dormitory was flooded. We were soaked. My friend didn't care. Physical trial was essential to her radical politics. If it didn't hurt in some way, then it didn't count as much. "We were so close," she moaned, suddenly, while I was patting her back. For a second there, I wasn't sure what she was talking about. McGovern had got trounced, losing every state except Massachusetts. "We came so close to changing this country," she sobbed through the blond hair plastered against her face.

But we—they—did change the country. A revolution in consciousness won and we ourselves live in our heads in a more open and accepting society. No one wants the social clock turned back, not even the conservatives who want to confine socially everyone except themselves. The 1960s are all over YouTube. The young are very aware that they live in a world that was changed by political protest and cultural challenge. No one ever thought we'd get this far, the elderly say.

I think of my father years ago, stopping by the supermarket where my brother-in-law is sitting at a voter registration table. I think of him going in search of my sisters at some other voter registration table on the other side of town to give them a message from my mother, and I vow to keep alive in my heart their defiance and hope. It is the best way for me to honor their memory, their local, brave actions, that state of grace the committed can become acquainted with.

WHAT BLACK MEANS NOW

IN "SPEAKING IN TONGUES," her stunning essay on Barack Obama and black identity, Zadie Smith remembers how convinced she was, as a student at Cambridge, by the concept of a unified black voice. Then the idea faded somehow into the injunction to "keep it real," an instruction that she found felt like being in a prison cell:

> It made Blackness a quality each individual black person was constantly in danger of losing. And almost anything could trigger the loss of one's Blackness: attending certain universities, an impressive variety of jobs, a fondness for opera, a white girlfriend, an interest in golf. And of course, any change in the voice.

It's absurd, looking back, she says, because black reality

has diversified. We're "black ballet dancers and black truck drivers and black presidents...and we all sing from our own hymn sheet."[1]

But recently, when I asked her—in connection with the Trayvon Martin case—if she still felt that way about the hymn sheet, Smith said maybe it wasn't possible, because there was so much hostility toward black people in the US. In England, she had thought more about class than race. In the US, she discovered that someone else can rush in and define you when you least expect it, making your being black part of an idea of blackness far outside yourself.

An armed Latino's suspicion that a tall, thin black youth in a hoodie in a gated community at night must be an intruder up to no good closes for me discussion about a post-racial society. Private citizens can now get on a warlike footing with crime, even if the images of the criminal in their heads are racist. Trayvon Martin's moment of instruction—as Henry Louis Gates Jr. calls the recognition scene when the black youth realizes that he or she is different, and that the white world sees black people as different, no matter how they feel inside—has a history, one that yanks everybody back a step.

It would seem that although black people are in the mainstream, black history still isn't, because certain basic things about the history of being black in America—

American history—have to be explained again and again. At the end of the Civil War, vast numbers of black men were on the roads looking for work, for sold-off family, for peace. In the late nineteenth century and into the twentieth, black men who could not prove employment or residence in a town that they happened to be passing through were imprisoned and put to work. Vagrancy laws were a form of social control, much like the war on drugs that Michelle Alexander in *The New Jim Crow* (2010)—such an important book—forcefully argues is today's extension of America's overseer-style management of black men. Drug laws have always been aimed at minorities.

In another brilliant work that tells us how directly the past has formed us, *The Condemnation of Blackness: Race, Crime, and the Making of Modern Urban America* (2010), Khalil Gibran Muhammad looks at the interpretation white social scientists have made of crime statistics since the 1890s that, as he says, stigmatized crime as black and masked white crime as individual failure. Crime was linked to blacks as a racial group, but not to whites. "Blackness was refashioned through crime statistics. It became a more stable racial category in opposition to whiteness through racial criminalization." Black criminality justified prejudice. Because it was thought that blacks could not be socialized, they were largely excluded from the social reform programs that in the 1920s were making immigrant groups American. Irish, Italian, and Polish immigrants, meanwhile, shed their criminal identities as groups, but blacks didn't.

Black America has fought back at certain times by embracing stereotypes and turning what have been regarded as cultural defects into cultural virtues. And white America has been riveted. The Jazz Age was, in part, a reaction to the slaughter of World War I. Many whites wanted to be primitive, to be an intuitive, emotional, musical, sexually uninhibited black, as opposed to a mechanistic and rational white. Sherwood Anderson's *Dark Laughter* (1925) ends with the black maids laughing at the cuckolded white boss. Similarly, the black urban thug of the 1950s became the existential Beat hero of the nihilistic atomic age celebrated by Norman Mailer in his essay "The White Negro." The riots of the 1960s politicized the hipster: the street criminal became the political prisoner; the black who would not fight for his country became the militant with ties to international revolution.

Ironically, the season of extreme black rhetoric in the 1970s coincided with the doubling of the size of the black middle class. New laws mandating equal employment opportunities brought rapid results for blacks. Yet blacks entering the middle class were still disadvantaged compared to middle-class whites. This was why many black critics found unconvincing William Julius Wilson's thesis in *The Declining Significance of Race* (1978)—that in the modern industrial system a black person's economic position shaped his or her life to a greater extent than did race—because it did not adequately address institutional racism, systemic inequality. In the 1970s, most black families needed two incomes to be middle-class. More black women had entered the middle class than black men, because secretarial and clerical work, though considered white-collar jobs, were also thought of as occupations for women. A black man had to have more education and be in a higher occupation in order to earn an income comparable to a white man.

In 1980, the top one hundred black businesses employed no more than nine thousand people. Since Reconstruction blacks had been ruthlessly excluded from mainstream business life. Ida B. Wells, whose Memphis newspaper, *Free Speech*, had been burned down in 1892, showed that lynching victims were often black men whose businesses whites wanted to take over. Of the 130 black banks founded since Emancipation, one remained by the Depression. During World War II, the largest white insurance company had more black customers than the forty-four black insurance companies combined. White intimidation, the discriminatory practices of white financial institutions as well as the inability to penetrate white markets, would cause most black businesses to fail. Those that survived were what sociologists called "defensive enterprises," which catered to personal needs—barbers, cleaners, tailors, restaurateurs, grocers—and set up in places where whites didn't want to operate. The only significant black manufacturers in America were those of skin lighteners, hair straighteners, and coffins.[2]

Since state and federal government programs were the primary source of middle-class growth for blacks in the 1960s and 1970s, Reagan-era cuts in government spending hit this segment of the black middle class hardest. Blacks made progress in the 1960s because it was the time of "the affluent society." Blacks were not in direct competition with whites for jobs. However, the recessions of the 1970s and 1980s brought furious opposition among whites to race-biased government policies.

The conservative backlash said that blacks ought to stop blaming white society for the predominance of single-parent households in black America headed by women, the sort of argument that made the social analyses in Andrew Hacker's *Two Nations: Black and White, Separate, Hostile, Unequal* (1992) something of a relief. Hacker noted that if a neighborhood became more than 10 percent black, then white flight ensued. Residential segregation determined the quality of the resources black people could get from grammar school to retirement. Many black people greeted former university presidents William G. Bowen and Derek Bok's *The Shape of the River* (1998) with elation. Their exhaustive survey of the long-term consequences of affirmative action supported race-sensitive recruitment in higher education, because American society needed black professionals. Moreover, they found that far from being ill equipped to compete in the open market, the beneficiaries of affirmative action were highly successful.

A subgenre of black autobiography emerged that documented the transition from one class to another: these books described the alienation of the black professional in the high-pressure workplace or the loneliness of the black scholarship student at the elite white school, as in Lorene Cary's *Black Ice* (1991), a beautiful memoir of her quest for self-acceptance at St. Paul's, in New Hampshire. In these works, the class voyagers see themselves as the equivalent of being culturally bilingual. Then, too, the debate between separatism and assimilation was going away. To join the system was enough of a challenge to that system. The old war cries that American society had to be remade in order to become equitable faded. Not only was the revolution not going to be televised; it was no longer coming.

Black nationalists in the 1960s and 1970s had been fierce in their judgments of those deemed Uncle Toms, so much so that black neoconservatives still saw themselves as the victims of a totalitarian black identity imposed by black radicals; they, the neoconservatives, were the brave new dissenters, the individualists. The old debate about separatism and integration was transformed into a discussion between pessimists, those who believed blacks would remain outsiders, and optimists/opportunists, those who believed in moving up by working from within. Insiders like Colin Powell and Condoleezza Rice supposedly vindicated faith in color-blind success in America. In 2003, *Forbes* magazine proclaimed Oprah Winfrey the country's first black woman billionaire. The cultural moment seemed fixated on narratives of ascent. But most of the black middle class was still a lower middle class, living paycheck to paycheck, without substantial assets.

Black colleges had created the old black professional class, a middle class flattered to be seen as an upper class, because truly upper-class blacks, such as Lena Horne's family, were so few. Traditionally, blacks already someplace tended to resent other blacks trying to crowd in. As St. Clair Drake and Horace R. Cayton reported in *Black Metropolis: A Study of Negro Life in a Northern City* (1945), blacks in Chicago who considered themselves "Old Settlers" blamed the devastating white riot against blacks in 1919 on new black arrivals from the South, saying that they destroyed the social balance between the races. Before the mass migration of blacks from the South, the thinking went, there had been plenty of jobs and little prejudice, because blacks had known how to behave. They didn't "make apes out of themselves," as one Old Settler civil engineer put it, still annoyed by the no-accounts almost a quarter of a century later.

Drake and Cayton pointed out that membership in the upper- or middle-class Negro world wasn't determined entirely by income or occupation. Family ties and especially education counted, as did the symbols or markers of middle-class identity: clothes and manners. "Middle-class organizations put the accent on 'front,' respectability, civic responsibility of a sort, and conventionalized recreation." It was the pretensions of the black upper strata that E. Franklin Frazier savaged in his famously ill-tempered essay, *Black Bourgeoisie*

(1957). The black upper class, he reminded everyone, was really only an upper middle class and considerably poorer in relation to the white upper middle class.

Frazier would not have been the only one frustrated by what he saw as the complacence of the black middle class at a critical moment in American history. Because of widespread discrimination in hiring practices, the black middle class hardly increased after the war, though the black GI Bill generation had come of age. It was the America of David Riesman's *The Lonely Crowd* (1950), his suburbs full of conformists, and Frazier was no less scornful of the materialism on the black side of town. He accused middle-class blacks of not wanting integration because they feared loss of their position. Drake and Cayton had made a similar charge against middle-class blacks in their study, an important work, but of its period in that "race leader" is identified as a middle-class occupation. The NAACP's rank and file was drawn from the black professional class, the self-employed who couldn't be threatened by white bosses, a black middle-class tradition Frazier does not describe.

For Frazier, the black middle class was an escapist elite and never mind that Thurgood Marshall, Martin Luther King Jr., and Andrew Young grew up in the black middle class or that the elderly black women in the Cottagers, an exclusive Oaks Bluffs club on Martha's Vineyard, were for the most part staunch supporters of civil rights. All through the 1960s and 1970s, middle-class life in America was mocked. That is an American tradition in itself. Amiri Baraka was stringent in his satire of middle-class blacks, but America went on measuring its social progress in upward mobility, in access to the middle class, and black people kept on wanting to move up.

Interestingly enough, not everyone considered black entry into the middle class the same thing as a victory for integration. That was a miscalculation on the part of black neoconservatives, who would be exasperated with Obama because he looked like them on paper but refused to repudiate the lessons of the civil rights era. Black America did not get a conservatism comparable to white political conservatism until the Fairmont Conference in 1980, which brought Clarence Thomas and Thomas Sowell to prominence as critics of civil rights "orthodoxy." Black neoconservatives received much attention for attacking the prestige of the civil rights movement, but it didn't work, because ever since the National Black Political Convention in Gary, Indiana, in 1972, convened by Baraka, among others, the benefits of blacks thinking of themselves as a voting bloc, the unified black voice, were obvious in those cities and congressional districts where to do so meant political gain.

Gangster rap and mellower styles of hip-hop have been with us for so long that we can forget the part the rap aesthetic has played in reconciling the black revolutionary imperative with the materialism of American society. The hero of Spike Lee's *Do the Right Thing* (1989) says over and over that he is just trying to "get paid," and hip-hop made "bling" cool not just in the ghetto but in middle-class America as well. Hip-hop crossed racial and class boundaries, its transgressive postures speaking to almost any young man in its orbit. What it told young black men was that success could be a kind of militancy and that it did not mean you had to act white or give up any of your yo dog whassup. Black students took their rap soundtrack with them to Harvard Law School. Blackness was portable. You could take your roots with you, just as Gertrude Stein had hoped.

During the first decade of the twenty-first century one out of four black men was or had been in prison, yet blacks were also seen in occupations they hadn't held before—stockbrokers, corporate attorneys, investment fund managers, CEOs of white companies. Black America was represented at all levels of society, however thin the numbers at the top. They could object to the assumption that success implied that they were traitors, as the Harvard law professor Randall Kennedy described the anxiety in *Sellout: The Politics of Racial Betrayal* (2008).

One of the magical elements of President Obama's rise was that no one had predicted it, in spite of Edward Brooke of Massachusetts and Douglas Wilder of Virginia, who had demonstrated that a culturally assimilated black candidate could appeal to white middle-class voters. Obama's victory was celebrated in the streets as a promise of American democracy fulfilled, and the triumphalism among the black professional class was astonishing. But this was history, a culmination, a turning point. Everyone could see the painful drama of succession as Jesse Jackson gazed on the president-elect. Since then, a new black elite has been trying to tell us—and themselves—where they stand in relation to black history. There are now so many of them that to be a middle-class black does not seem as elitist as it used to be. The black elite of one generation gets replaced by the black elite of another, the later one defined by different criteria, including a greater sense of freedom.

The black poor are not the ones who are trying to

redefine black America. In *Disintegration: The Splintering of Black America* (2010), Eugene Robinson, a writer for *The Washington Post*, argues that the pre–civil rights one-nation black America doesn't exist anymore and that blacks have little in common apart from symbols left over from their civil rights history. Robinson takes it as a given that the blacks of the "mainstream" are now middle-class:

> Because of desegregation and disintegration, the black middle class is not only bigger and wealthier but also liberated from the separate but unequal nation called black America that existed before the triumph of civil rights. The black Mainstream is now woven into the fabric of America, not just economically but culturally as well.

The Bureau of Labor Statistics reported in 2010 that the median income of blacks had fallen from $32,584 to $29,328, compared to the national median income of $49,777. While 43.7 percent of whites were categorized as middle-class, the percentage of the black population that was middle-class was 38.4 percent. Almost 29 percent of the black population was called working-class and 23.5 percent was described as living in poverty.

Robinson renames the black classes: the Emergent,

meaning African immigrants who now outperform Asian students at the university level; the Abandoned, or the underclass, as they have been called, blacks trapped by low income in neighborhoods and schools where it is impossible to project a decent future; the Mainstream, who may work in integrated settings but still lead socially all-black lives; and the Transcendent, "a small but growing cohort with the kind of power, wealth, and influence that previous generations of African Americans could never have imagined."

Robinson hopes that the Transcendent class will provide leaders, much as W. E. B. Du Bois had called on his Talented Tenth more than a century ago, but Robinson's expectations contradict his own evidence that blacks don't feel race solidarity the way they used to. He cites a 2007 Pew poll that said 61 percent of blacks don't believe that the black poor and the black middle class share common values.

To judge from Touré's confident *Who's Afraid of Post-Blackness?: What It Means to Be Black Now* (2011), the Transcendent are keen to inform America that what it means to be black has changed for them. Touré, a *Rolling Stone* and MSNBC contributor, CNN popular culture correspondent, and apostle of the hip-hop aesthetic, contends that there are now as many ways to be black as there are black individuals. Touré was born in 1971. His generation may have missed the heroic civil rights era, but he claims they are at ease in the decentralized world of new media and competitive branding. They are liberated by Obama's example; "authentic" and "inauthentic" no longer apply:

> The definitions and boundaries of Blackness are expanding in forty million directions—or really, into infinity. It does not mean that we are leaving Blackness behind, it means we're leaving behind the vision of Blackness as something narrowly definable and we're embracing every conception of Blackness as legitimate. Let me be clear: Post-Black does not mean "post-racial." Post-racial posits that race does not exist or that we're somehow beyond race and suggests colorblindness: It's a bankrupt concept that reflects a naive understanding of race in America. Post-Black means we are like Obama: rooted in but not restricted by Blackness.

Touré interviews 105 black people, mostly men, some older than he, and most from Robinson's Transcendent sphere: politicians such as former Congressman Harold Ford Jr. of Tennessee; rap stars like Chuck D of Public

Enemy; writers, including Greg Tate, Nelson George, and Malcolm Gladwell; academics such as Henry Louis Gates Jr., Cornel West, and Patricia J. Williams; and artists like Kara Walker, Glenn Ligon, and Kehinde Wiley, among others. The majority of his interviewees are "identity liberals," legatees of Zora Neale Hurston's refusal to see her work as being always in the service of mournful racial uplift.

They recall the "nigger wake-up call," Touré's sensationalistic term for Gates's moment of instruction. Several of these stories involve the police. Most have to do with coming up against the matter-of-fact power of whiteness. For example, Derek Conrad Murray, an art history professor at the University of California, Santa Cruz, remembers when his father, a hospital administrator, moved the family to an exclusive suburb of Seattle in the early 1980s. His intensely Catholic family was the only black family that attended mass at a large church in the area. One Sunday, a mentally unstable parishioner stood and yelled, "You niggers should get out of here!" Murray said his father chased the man into the street and nearly choked him to death. The shock to the family was such that nobody ever went to church or prayed again. Murray became an atheist.

Touré comments that these stories are not just about whites attempting to break black spirit; they are also

about black resiliency. Touré's subjects sometimes remember a harrowing racial experience and then declare
that the lesson they took away was their determination
to be as free personally as possible. They claim for
themselves the unencumbered psychological freedom
that several young black politicians appropriate for
themselves in Gwen Ifill's *The Breakthrough: Politics
and Race in the Age of Obama* (2009). Everyone knows
that having a black president means something. People
are knocking themselves out to explain just what. But
it's too soon.

The black people who seem most free in Touré's book
are the visual artists. Indeed, "post-blackness" was a
term coined in the late 1990s by Thelma Golden, the
director and chief curator of the Studio Museum in
Harlem, and the conceptual artist Glenn Ligon to describe "the liberating value in tossing off the immense
burden of race-wide representation, the idea that everything they do must speak to or for or about the entire
race." Black culture is a subject matter, but the new
black artists don't treat it as "specific to them." It is not
autobiographical. It is an interest, not a weapon.

   While it is obviously true that Kehinde Wiley, one of
the hottest artists in New York, is very different from

the black artists Jacob Lawrence or Romare Bearden in his attitude toward his subjects, Wiley still draws on black history, black images. Similarly, Touré's short stories in *The Portable Promised Land* (2002) and his novel, *Soul City* (2004), are allegories written in a black jive that has lost none of its connection to the past and depends on it for meaning. Many critics have made the point that white America has no trouble taking black culture on board while leaving black people out in the cold.

Touré urges black people to claim the freedom of the artist. This message from James Baldwin's fiction is hardly new. Touré has little to say about the "new Jim Crow" that has put so many poor young blacks in prison. For him, blackness is above all about style. His interviewees stress the importance of not internalizing society's messages about blackness, a dictum that goes back to Marcus Garvey. What's new is not knowing whether racism is behind the hassles that come up in daily life for a black person. Nelson George: "Now, if they show you their ass somehow then you have to decide whether this is racism or it's because they're assholes."

Touré asserts that much of black America did not share white America's outrage at the attack on the World Trade Center in 2001: "A spoiled country getting the comeuppance it deserved." Many whites may also have felt this "emotional distance," just as many blacks were, indeed, grief-stricken. But then Touré moves quickly on to his main point: the end of ambivalence about being American for blacks like him. "We are American. And we are so American that rejecting this country means rejecting part of ourselves."

Historically, Pan-Africanism has been a component of American black nationalism, but Touré makes it clear that his generation isn't looking to Africa as their source of black identity, a major generational difference:

> Black Americans and Africans are speaking differ-ent languages when it comes to race because of his-tories on different sides of slavery and the Atlantic....We are, like jazz, rock 'n roll, and hip-hop, a child of Africa molded by distinctly Ameri-can longings, joys, and pains as well as uniquely shaped by being in America.

Touré's parents grew up under segregation in the projects in Brooklyn, "with laws and society arrayed to attempt to keep them boxed in to niggerdom." But they reared their family in a middle-class suburb of Boston. Touré went to private school, where he played tennis and was not the only black kid in his classes. "I grew up in an integrated world without racist laws holding me back." Now Touré lives in a hip, mixed section of Brooklyn, has married outside the faith, as he puts it, and is socially relaxed enough that when his toddler dived into a piece of watermelon he trusted that his white friends were laughing because children do cute things, not because a pickaninny displayed the response to watermelon that they as whites had been conditioned to expect.

Touré represents the anti-essentialist idea of blackness, a discourse of privilege, far from the race feeling that said if it happens to one of us, it happens to all of us. But I remember what it is like, wanting to break away from categories not of your own devising. I told myself that I would not become one of those old heads who says, In my day... Still, I find myself thinking back to my youth, when not long after Martin Luther King was killed my sister tried to tell me about a cousin of my mother's who was lynched in 1930. I didn't want to hear it. I fled. I got away from that contagious form of blackness, the historical truth.

Then a few years later, I read J. Saunders Redding's *On Being Negro in America* (1951), a book from Elizabeth Hardwick's shelves. Redding, by then a prim professor, remembered that when he was at Atlanta University in 1930, he armed himself after a classmate,

Dennis Hubert, was lynched because he'd been seen talking to a white girl. The name of my mother's cousin rushed toward my eyes. I phoned home. My mother had been six years old when it happened. She recalled that her mother was wearing a blue dress. She left the house suddenly...

(*The New York Review of Books*, May 24, 2012)

BUCK MOON IN HARLEM

I WILL LOOK for you in the stories of new kings. Juneteenth isn't mentioned in the writings of W. E. B. Du Bois or Carter Woodson, the founder of *The Journal of Negro History*. I haven't yet come across a description of the first Juneteenth celebrations equivalent to Colonel Thomas Wentworth Higginson's report of the ceremonies for the Emancipation Proclamation as it was read aloud on Port Royal Island, South Carolina, on New Year's Day, 1863. Black troops, white commanders, white clergymen, white women schoolteachers, black women schoolteachers, and the formerly enslaved turned resisters gathered at the sober campground to ratify in their hearts the next covenant of the Republic.

Various sources tell us that when news of Robert E. Lee's surrender in Virginia reached the West a few weeks later, the Confederate army in Texas began to fall apart. Even so, federal authority depended on the presence of Union troops. In his memoirs, Ulysses S. Grant remembers that General Gordon Granger charged with "such a roar of musketry" at the Battle of Chattanooga that the rebels heard him from a long way off and had time to get away. When Grant learned that Granger had turned up in New Orleans, the War Department ignored his advice that the general not be given another command. Granger arrived in Galveston, Texas, on June 19, 1865, to announce and enforce the Emancipation Proclamation. Texas was the last Confederate state to be occupied.

Surprise is an essential element of beauty, the poets say, and several arresting minutes of silent film shot by Reverend S.S. Jones in Oklahoma City in 1925 have been making the Internet rounds of late. His stationary camera captures a Juneteenth parade, a bold march of heartbreakingly well-dressed black people—marching bands, Pullman porters, black women's clubs under large black umbrellas, and black veterans of both World War I and the Spanish-American War. They are moving through a residential neighborhood where we see scarcely any spectators, as if everyone who lived on that tidy street were in the parade. Juneteenth was a black holiday out West, not down South, I assumed, and therefore not a memory that traveled with black people

in their migrations to the cities of the Northeast and
Midwest in the first half of the twentieth century. Ob-
servance of Juneteenth supposedly fell off over time. It
was revived nationally in the Black Expo days of the
1970s, when Kwanzaa was first catching on as the Afri-
canist Christmas.

I'd not heard of Juneteenth until Ralph Ellison's long-
awaited second novel was published posthumously in
1999.[1] *Juneteenth* is mostly voice, or voices, "in the be-
loved idiom," as Ellison said. It centers on the confron-
tation between a white senator and the black preacher
who taught him when still a boy how to hold a crowd.
The Ellisonian twist is that the racist senator may have
been brought up as a black boy. The novel opens in the
1950s and flashes back to the senator's childhood with
the preacher on the black revival circuit in the South
before World War I and his escape across the color line
as a roving white filmmaker in the Southwest sometime
in the 1920s. Ellison's rhetorical invention reaches its
climax as the senator and preacher remember, sepa-
rately and together, a Juneteenth celebration on a hot,
dusty night in a tent in rural Alabama, not out West.

Old-fashioned Negroes getting Emancipation mixed
up with the Resurrection and vaudeville, the senator
thinks at first. The preacher remembers the workers in
white uniforms, barrels of ice, yellow cases of soda pop,

the vast quantities of catfish and ham, coleslaw and chocolate cake. At the sunrise services, they were "playing for *keeps*." The preacher is dismayed that his former prodigy could have forgotten how in their sermon they invoked the Middle Passage and its images of tongues cut out and talking drums stolen. One group can't be given license to kill another in order to prove their superiority, he thinks to himself. He carries scars from the fights he got into trying to go to the polls in Oklahoma armed with ax handles and pistols, and accompanied by some Native American and white sympathizers. Ellison has maybe given his preacher a fighting past he wished he'd had himself. But then his preacher suspects that whites were attempting to destroy the humility of black people because they had sensed its life-preserving power, as if Ellison had to reposition him so that his Juneteenth peroration emphasizes how blacks sang and danced, survived and flourished.

Ellison opposed the notion of black life as a "metaphysical condition" of "irremediable agony" because that made it seem as though it either took place in a vacuum or had only one theme. In his writings about the jazz greats he heard play in his youth in Oklahoma, he gives them credit for expressing something about the optimism of blacks as a group that found no definition elsewhere. Ellison recalled with pride his music teacher, who had her students join the Scottish reel competition on May Day, ignoring people who said black students ought not to learn European folk dances. Black people coming from enslaved circumstances couldn't cling to their cultural idioms and survive; therefore they sought to extend their range, Ellison claimed. Cultural synthesis was important to "the unnoticed logic of the democratic process." He insisted that segregation had not cut off black people from various fields of influence and that in turn American culture was marked at every point by black vernacular culture. This mixture was an opportunity, as he saw it, a chance to make a humanly richer society.

Ellison, born in 1913, made much of the pioneer spirit shared between black and white, and it mattered to him that Oklahoma had not been a part of the Confederacy. Though blacks by law had the vote, Oklahoma's state constitution in 1907 forbade integrated schools and classified as "colored" anyone with any degree of black blood, while Native Americans were classed as "white." The state legislature found means to keep black people from voting. Ellison was only eight years old when in 1921 in Tulsa a black youth, Dick Rowland, was arrested for supposedly assaulting a white woman in a downtown elevator. Armed black men protecting the prisoner in the county jail turned back a white mob, after which white people went on a rampage, destroying Greenwood, the thriving black business section, looting, burning black homes, running black people out of town. Seventy black people were killed and nine white people.

In 1930, in Chickasha, Oklahoma, a black youth—Henry Argo—was arrested for the rape of a white girl and the attempted murder of her child. It was rumored that Argo and the girl were lovers. A mob of two thousand white men attacked the jail with battering rams, drove off the National Guard with gunfire, used commandeered National Guard equipment to pull the jail doors off their hinges, smashed a hole through the concrete cell that held Argo, shot him, and stabbed him. He bled to death on his way to a hospital in Oklahoma City.

In her autobiography, *A Matter of Black and White* (1996), Ada Lois Sipuel Fisher recalls that in her family the story was that the mob came back for Henry Argo only after the sheriff had assured the armed black men guarding the jailhouse that he was no longer in danger. There had been talk of parading his body through the black part of town to teach them a lesson. The town's one black doctor gathered together bootleggers and gamblers—"this was no job for church folks—and declared that any white man who crossed Minnesota

Street with that boy's body would die in colored town."
Whether the story of black anger was legend or not,
Sipuel notes that Argo's murder was the last recorded
lynching in the state.

Sipuel's parents had moved to Chickasha shortly after
the riot in Tulsa, where black men like her father—a
Pentecostal minister—who tried to protect black prop-
erties got rounded up by white militias. There were no
parks or playgrounds for black children in Chickasha
when Sipuel was growing up in the 1920s. After she
graduated from Langston University in 1945, the only
state-supported college open to black students in Oklahoma, Sipuel volunteered to join Thurgood Marshall's
NAACP challenge to the state's segregation laws by ap-
plying to the all-white University of Oklahoma law
school—the only public law school in the state. In *Sipuel
v. Board of Regents of the University of Oklahoma*
(1948), the Supreme Court agreed with the argument
that the state had to provide her with a law education
under the equal protection clause of the Fourteenth
Amendment. Sipuel's case was a precursor of *Brown* v.
Board of Education.

So that was Frederick Douglass's portrait on the cover
of the September 1963 issue of *Ebony* magazine

commemorating the one hundredth anniversary of the Emancipation Proclamation. He didn't look like any black man we'd yet seen in Indianapolis, Indiana, not with that hair. Douglass, to me, looked like Mark Twain. My mother confiscated *The Prince and the Pauper*. I'd flubbed her oral examination on Arna Bontemps's biography for young people, *Frederick Douglass*. I had a presentation to make on Douglass at the club for black children that my poor mother had us participate in, bored though she was by its activities, she later confessed. History making your hands shake before apple bobbing on your knees with your hands behind your back.

It felt natural, my separate and unequal education of the history I learned at home, constituting mostly what my parents had read when they were students at black colleges, and the history I was taught at mostly white schools, a curriculum aimed at the Advanced Placement exam on, say, Richard Hofstadter's passionate studies of American political ideas or the history of populism, works in which black people do not figure. When the young historian Vincent Harding said early on in the Black Power movement that he wanted nothing less than the reinterpretation of the entire American past, he sounded like another hothead black nationalist utopian.

February is Black History Month because it's the

shortest month, we used to laugh. But Carter G. Woodson launched Negro History Week in February 1926 because both Lincoln and Douglass were born in February, their birthdays long celebrated in black communities. Then every month became Black History Month, to judge from the advance bookings—pre-pandemic— at the National Museum of African American History in Washington, D.C. David Adaye's magnificent ark drew one off the Mall toward its doors. What made the exhibits bearable—here were wall screens of interviews with Tulsa survivors—was that the structure was as busy with souls as a cathedral.

The weirdness was elsewhere, I was telling myself back in February. My aunt in Massachusetts, a long-retired middle school teacher, was perplexed that her favorite Chinese restaurant was completely deserted, except for us. On my first visit to her little town near Fort Devens, where her husband had been reassigned, her history lesson was about the soldiers who came back to Fort Devens in 1918 with Spanish flu, and it spread from there. Fort Devens is long closed, phantoms snuck through my aunt's window and replaced the thermostat she loved with an inferior one, and it was a further measure of her dementia that sitting there over egg rolls too rubbery to tear, she had never heard of influenza at Devens. It has been a measure of her dementia in the past few months that her understanding of Covid-19 remains on a par with that of seemingly everyone in the White House.

On March 16, New York City woke to learn that schools, restaurants, theaters, and concert venues would be closed. In the unpredicted schedule of gyms shuttered next and speaker-loaded squad cars roaming my neighborhood to warn people to maintain social distance, in the unprecedented drama of self-isolation and quarantine followed by lockdown, angry noncompliance among black people was a clue as to how vulnerable we were in the pandemic. My trainer, a young black family man who saved himself from the streets, speculated that Covid was a Chinese invention for the trade war, but it backfired. In the face of mounting evidence about how, in lieu of a vaccine, social behavior mattered in dealing with the virus, my trainer, already streaming workout sessions, was adamant that he was more afraid of the police than he was of the pandemic. Chicago's black mayor, Lori Lightfoot, found it necessary to denounce the social media myth that black people could not get infected.

The class character of the pandemic was soon very clear anyway—who worked in what were deemed essential services, who had to show up on those front lines, who had to keep packing and delivering, whom they were going home to, who had poor health in the first place and often inadequate health care. By mid-April in some states, black people made up a much higher percentage of confirmed cases than the percentage of black people in the general population. Black people were 40 percent of Covid sufferers in Michigan, while only 14 percent of the population. "Liberate Michigan," immortal white people in Lansing chanted against strict lockdown. The pandemic was showing us that most of us had never had to do this before—merely survive.

Empty streets as a shared global experience, cleaner air, surveillance anxiety, loss of livelihood, disturbances in overcrowded prisons, hospital staff martyrs, double bunking in the graveyards, and nightly salutes to workers, soldiers, and volunteers in danger also underscored how small is the man trying to hold our national destiny hostage to his sour vanity. Drink bleach, inject bleach, rise by Easter. If a person cannot imagine a future, then we would say that that person is depressed. But if a country cannot envision a future, how do we describe its condition? My partner said Republican Party policy was simply: "You can go back to work and you can die."

By May Day, the stay-at-home order in the city was

beginning to crumble. Footage would appear on social media of, say, an incident in Brooklyn in which the police had used social distancing guidelines as the reason to get rough with black guys hanging out in groups on sidewalks and between parked cars. They almost followed a script: disperse, why, disperse, no, stand-off, push, push back, take down. Then it happened.

Say his name
George Floyd

The pandemic dramatized what inequality looks like, and the police killing of George Floyd showed everyone what being black in America feels like, over and over again. Young America blew the lid off lockdown, a blast wave of outrage that reached around the world. Jill Nelson told Henry Louis Gates Jr. years ago that she was tired of going to all-black or mostly black demonstrations for social justice, that it was time for white people to show up. They did: their vast numbers are what Occupy Wall Street and Ferguson have led to, in part. Sustained public protest, staying in the streets, those who shall not be moved, taking over the mainstream narrative, if you want to talk that way, the coming together of opposition, if you prefer. Black Lives Matter was ready.

———

"Seize the time," posters said. I turned away from the demonstration at Lenox Avenue and West 125th Street after only fifteen minutes on the last Saturday afternoon in May. I couldn't hear the speeches and was too fearful after three months inside to wade into the warm crowd of a few hundred, even if everyone was wearing masks. I learned of demonstrations all over the city as the day went on, from Times Square to Union Square, back to Trump Tower, and for a second night things were hot around the Barclays Center in Brooklyn. One friend called the police about a redneck's truck with Florida license plates parked overnight on East 12th Street. High-end sneakers went first in Soho, I was told, and white girls were spotted racing out of a jewelry shop. Electronics stores in Union Square got trashed, but the Strand Bookstore was untouched. Practiced black gangs wearing do-rags hit lush life windows all the way up Madison Avenue after the cops rolled on.

The Third Precinct in Minneapolis had been set on fire the previous night; Atlanta protesters jumped police cars and shattered glass. LA and Orange County erupted in protests five hundred years in the making, my cousin said by text. "All the Power to the People!" Peaceful by day, chaotic when the sun went down, protests continued to spread across the country into 140 cities. Each seemed to gather up the names of black youth murdered by police (Breonna Taylor in Louisville, back in March) or by racist white assailants (Ahmaud Arbery in south Georgia, back in February) and to sift through the more than five thousand names in *The Washington Post*'s database of fatal police shootings since 2015. Amazed, I watched video of a police car burning at Monument Circle in Indianapolis, where my family marched in 1961. Two people had been shot in the area, but it wasn't clear by whom.

Back in the Sixties, black leaders were under pressure to condemn riots, summer after summer. The leaders of old and new civil rights groups were placed on a spectrum of nonviolent to violent, as in who can be reasoned with. In 1992, after the unrest provoked by the Rodney King verdict, some were saying that images of marauding black people allowed federal and state government to dodge the issue of police violence. However, enough protesters in 2020 were not to be detained by old-style fretting over the difference between rebellion and riot, or what broken glass left behind psychologically in black neighborhoods. Young protesters quoted Reverend King, who spoke of riots as "the voice of the unheard." Michael McDowell, a founder of BLM Minneapolis, explained in an interview online that it

was futile for local authorities to try to control community reaction to the murder of George Floyd. Lost property could be replaced, but not a life.

I was more trapped in my own script of protective,
evasively moral responses than I had realized. A jour-
nalist friend covering the pandemic and its consequences
in Brazil was shocked that I'd say I mourned the black
man robbed of his life, yet waste pity on the cop who
ignored his dying pleas or on the other cops who stood
by. They're not the dead ones, she said, and a white supremacist gun culture in Brazil had let the police kill
177 youths in the favelas of Rio in the month of April
alone. The demonstrations and riots were part of the
same movement and did wonders to bring policing and
racial inequality into global discussion, I had to admit.
The world was taking a knee. The sheer scale and brutal directness of what was going on urged me to look
inward at my own symptoms of the philistine terror of
change.

It's not that there are no leaders, there is almost no need
for one, because everyone is a leader in a decentralized
network of contacts, alliances, affinity groups, with
varied agendas. "ANTIFA will fight cops," observed
Reverend Osagyefo Sekou, my guardian and guide in

Ferguson six years ago. ANTIFA descends from the Black Block at antiglobalization protests in the 1990s. Anarchists dressed in black; "it is not an organization," Reverend Sekou noted. "It is a position, a political disposition."

In his introduction to *The Making of Black Lives Matter: A Brief History of an Idea* (2017), Christopher J. Lebron observes:

Eschewing traditional hierarchical leadership models, the movement cannot be identified with any single leader or small group of leaders, despite the role [Patrisse] Cullors, [Opal] Tometi, and [Alicia] Garza played in giving us the social movement hashtag that will likely define our generation. Rather, #BlackLivesMatter represents an ideal that motivates, mobilizes, and informs the actions and programs of many local branches of the movement. Much like the way a corporate franchise works, minus revenue and profit, #BlackLivesMatter is akin to a social movement brand that can be picked up and deployed by any interested group of activists inclined to speak out and act against racial injustice.

Thousands of protesters demanded that police forces be defunded and disarmed and an end to lynching by proxy. The city council of Minneapolis agreed, and voted to disband its department. No other city has followed its lead. Many find, say, New York City mayor Bill de Blasio's defunding proposals disappointing, yet the mass appeal of such proposals, their quick endorsement by well-intentioned mayors and even some police chiefs, confirmed what Black Lives Matter had been telling us since Trayvon Martin's gun-stupid murderer was acquitted in 2013. The "prophetic storyline" was moving on. The George Floyd Justice in Policing Act— passed by the House but not, of course, by the Senate— would end qualified immunity and racial profiling, ban chokeholds and no-knock warrants, limit the amount of military equipment in police department arsenals, and require officers to wear body cameras. Lynching would become a hate crime, one hundred years after the Senate failed to pass the Dyer Anti-Lynching Bill. De Blasio told the demonstrators they'd won, they could go home, but they weren't listening. If it wasn't going to be OK to break lockdown to hang out in bars, then it had to be more than OK to go to a demo, and the killing hadn't stopped.

Court-decreed integration and affirmative action were twentieth-century social engineering solutions that the federal government in the near future and for some time to come most likely will be constrained to pursue. By the end of the twentieth century, programs designed to achieve such aims were being written off in some quarters as palliatives that failed to address the "time-release social debilitations" stemming from slavery. If the US is suffering, and the systemic racism of society is the underlying condition, then here is the cure: get rid of systemic racism. For its supporters, reparations are the twenty-first century's farewell to the twentieth century and its problems of the color line, a financial reset button, a persuasive form of white atonement, a vindication of those black nationalist pamphlets about the promise of forty acres and a mule to the formerly enslaved that the Union never honored.

These days people speak of equity, not equality. Nobody is waiting around for a government apology for founding atrocities when meaningful compensation would say a great deal more. The cost of reparations usually has been put in implausible-sounding trillions, but Robert F. Smith, the chairman of Vista Equity Partners, an intensely successful black investment firm that specializes in technology, has proposed a plan by which large corporations, particularly banks, would, given their racist histories of exclusionary and predatory practices, set aside 2 percent of their net income for a decade to support and create black businesses. In his address to this year's Forbes 400 Summit, Smith "pointed out that the net income of the ten largest US banks over the last ten years was $968 billion." Two percent of that would be $19.14 billion, which could fund "the core Tier 1 capital of community development banks and minority depository institutions." His 2 percent plan would also train students from black colleges for the telecom and tech sectors and digitize minority businesses.

That debate among twentieth-century civil rights organizations about whether to chart full citizenship by concentrating on economic advancement or winning political rights is obsolete, and so, too, is the argument about change from within or knocking the whole thing down. The struggle has always been waged on several fronts, and unevenly. The response to the death of George Floyd has also been shaped by black people in positions of influence. Their presence in the corporate, political, cultural, and educational institutions being asked to examine their systemic racism might be interpreted as a form of reparative capital. If our institutions are to hold together, it will be because minorities are insiders. "Love your community by voting," Smith, the financial activist, said.

LeBron James announced the formation of More Than a Vote, a nonprofit organization that would not only encourage African-Americans to vote, but use its "high-profile social media platform" to combat voter suppression. James's group would not endorse candidates but would seek to make the electoral process itself less intimidating to those who may have felt alienated from or outside it. James envisioned online tutorials, an idea reminiscent of the Voter Education Project, a private initiative established after the passage of the Voting Rights Act in 1965 that sent volunteers south to show new black voters how to fill out a ballot. Run by Vernon Jordan, the VEP turned out political landscape–changing numbers in many places in the South in the 1966 elections, and record numbers of black candidates won election nationwide.

Our Time Is Now: Power, Purpose, and the Fight for a Fair America, the Georgia politician Stacey Abrams's blueprint for where we need to be headed, was published in the middle of the suspended reality of the stealth virus wrecking the economy, and it helped to renew popular discussion about voting as a way to implement change, our rescue, at last. Abrams remembers that the Voting Rights Act was undermined wherever possible, and her grandparents in Mississippi couldn't vote until 1968. She describes her parents, both ministers, as coveted "super-voters," people who never miss an election, no matter how small. Yet she wonders if she had been brought up on the civil rights mythology about the magic of registration. Her campaign for governor of Georgia in 2018 taught her that to cast a ballot was not always the same as getting it counted. Voter suppression is not new in US history: "Brokers of power have sought to aggregate authority to themselves." Voter ID laws may have replaced bull whips, but the goal remains to discourage voting. A notary public's fee to certify an absentee ballot is a revived poll tax.

Abrams pronounces the guilt of founding documents—the Constitution, the Naturalization Act of 1790—in the long history of trying to control who belongs to the country, who has access to citizenship. In 1868 the passage of the Fourteenth Amendment made anyone born in the US a citizen, but not Native Americans. The Fifteenth Amendment gave black men the right to vote, but not black women and white women. States administered elections, and when Union troops were withdrawn from the South in the Compromise of 1876 the battle gained momentum to defeat the political power black people exercised during Reconstruction. It was a long walk to the Voting Rights Act of 1965, and though it took a while to take effect, Abrams says it changed black lives. It was effective because any jurisdiction mandated to be under its authority had to get the approval of the Justice Department for any alteration in election procedures. This was the provision for automatic compliance that the Supreme Court eviscerated in the 2013 decision *Shelby County v. Holder.*

As she goes through the intricacies of her confrontations with and mastery of electoral law, Abrams also manages to put faces to the forces of white supremacist opposition, those people against expanded voter rolls, felons' rights to vote, absentee ballots, mail-in ballots, early voting, same-day registration—policymaking clerks, collusive state judges, biased secretaries of state, all abusing their offices to remove people from registration lists, disqualify applicants, purge databases, conjure up fantasy voter fraud. "Voter identification," she writes, "is directly connected to suppression because the ID *is* a voter's access card to the polls." But then you have to get to a polling station and there has to *be* a polling station. Between the 2012 and 2016 elections, Abrams writes, the Election Assistance Commission reported that some three thousand polling sites had been closed. In much of America, race is the strongest predictor of political leanings. Who gets in matters. Ever the inspirer, John Lewis referred to the secular act of voting as "almost sacred." Abrams notes:

> Voting is an act of faith. It is profound. In a democracy, it is the ultimate power. Through the vote, the poor can access financial means, the infirm can

find health care supports, and the burdened and heavy-laden can receive a measure of relief from a social safety net that serves all. And we are willing to go to war to defend the sacred.

The crime of being black while walking—maybe the expression cuts across class lines, because it often depends on which coded costume of blackness is seen trespassing where, but the civil unrest under the klieg lamps gave blacks and whites the chance to make their bodies political and to know something of what black feminists in the Seventies, such as the Combahee River Collective cited by Abrams, meant when they talked about using the common experiences of identity as new organizing strategies. Interestingly enough, when many people are saying that the time has come to talk openly about class in the US, Abrams blames the concentration on class for holding back the development of an identity politics that relates more to the "intersections" that governed her life growing up. She looks to an identity-based new majority coalition of the nonwhite, women, and LGBTQ, and offers statistics showing that the number of voters in these categories will continue to be larger than we're used to thinking.

Our complex and unfinished history can be an impediment to the task of building solidarity and coalitions across racial lines when simplistically approached. Racism is one of those subjects that gives the feeling that there is no end to what you can find out once you start reading. Ralph Ellison never wrote about Booker T. Washington coming in 1905 to Boley, Oklahoma, one of many all-black towns founded by groups of black families determined to build better lives. Washington went back to Tuskegee and extolled the racial cooperation that the existence of such incorporated entities implied. Almost as soon as the words were out of his mouth, white bands attacked dozens of black towns, emptying many of them permanently. Ellison would insist that laughter enabled black people to cope and to deal with subjects they otherwise couldn't go near. Some days in the overwhelming news of demonstrations, it seemed that a new generation was bidding farewell to an old black trope: laughter to keep from crying. No more indirection for me. The folk adage "Don't let them see you suffer" turned into "*No mas.*"

This year, fireworks and firecrackers started in Harlem days before Juneteenth. They would begin early and go on all night. Explosions set off automobile alarms. The whisper of faraway rockets made me tense. Nearby, some whistled before they hit the asphalt. I stopped going to windows to see if I could spy colorful displays. "It sounds like small arms fire," my partner said one night in the dark. "It sounds like Tet," he said on another night, suddenly awake. In the middle of the night, it can smell like fire.

This was protest, defiance, keeping the movement going; celebration, misbehaving, power. This was the 24/7 of twenty-first-century talking drums. Many people were remembering Frederick Douglass's fierce address delivered in Rochester on July 5, 1852, "The Meaning of July Fourth for the Negro." He told the white citizens of the US that July 1776 was the "first great fact" in the nation's history, yet he had nothing to do with it, because the principles of political freedom and natural justice embodied in the Declaration of Independence did not extend to him or the people he represented. "This Fourth of July is *yours*, not *mine*." Slavery made a lie of the country's principles. Douglass said that he would rather stand with God and the crushed slave than argue anymore that a barbarous, shameless system was wrong: "At a time like this, scorching irony, not convincing argument, is needed."

Juneteeth as I hear it in Harlem and read it in greetings from friends and relatives—Happy Juneteenth Weekend!—is the black Fourth of July, or even the new Fourth of July. "It shall be Jubilee for you," we read in the Bible chapter devoted to the repackaging of rules and recommendations thousands of years old. I would not refuse the gift of one of those rare sixteenth-century silver Jubilee hammer heads with which every fifty years popes knocked on the sealed doors of St. Peter's; nevertheless, in the black Protestant church the Day of Jubilee sounds too old-timey and might have to go the darkie way of Aunt Jemima. A protective rope can be thrown around the noble Fisk Jubilee Singers. Juneteenth replaces the solemnity of Emancipation Day. A festival feeling recognizes in Lincoln's proclamation the instrument of war the Confederacy took it to be. The pieties of Emancipation have been outgrown. Gratitude for deliverance has dried up.

"Have some black culture. You'll feel better." Kevin Sweeney, a young filmmaker living in Santa Monica, California, observed that black culture and tech are among the biggest exports the US produces. "White America loves itself some black culture, it just doesn't love black people. Still." Although they wouldn't seem to do so at first, given the anger boldly and clumsily on display, the numerous Instagram posts of conciliatory gestures and messages, the rush of seemingly every business, educational, arts, and religious institution to advertise or seek guidance for measures that would eradicate systemic racism, suggest that if the nation is ill, then an accelerated process of cultural integration should be pre-scribed. The multiracial citizenry will not go uncounted. The not-normal nightly noise goes on. Either June-teenth in Harlem never ended or block after block finds it necessary to warn the demons that lured to Mount Rushmore total fools of personal whiteness. How wrong of me to gloat over Instagram photos of the former CEO of Godfather's Pizza at Tulsa's failed rally crowded close together with other faces of @Black Voices for Trump. Black people had crossed a threshold of pain, we were told, and white people and Latino people were crossing over with them; time was not going to save the Robert E. Lee Memorial in Richmond any longer. Confederate monuments were not, after all, slumberous.

July Fourth in Harlem is watched over by that envi-ous moon. Someone's antlers somewhere in the canceled city may be full. I, however, am waiting for the partial penumbral lunar eclipse promised by the CNN website. Is it lightning or fireworks, rain or rapid firecrackers, slow cloud or the earth's thin shadow? The Buck Moon outwaits me, and here on my screen are new names to learn: Li Wenliang, and then Joshua Wong, Agnes Chow, Shu Kei, Nathan Law, Isaac Cheng. *We must act out our freedom*, one masked, unnamed girl said in English to a camera during demonstrations on the anniversary of Hong Kong's handover to China.

Late, I open an e-mail from Kevin's uncle, John Sweeney, an attorney in Los Angeles who specializes in prosecuting excessive police force cases. He sent to the family the National Public Radio video of five teenage descendants of Frederick Douglass reciting passages from "The Meaning of July Fourth for the Negro." John noted that he plans to play the haunting video as his family prayer before dinner. Isidore Dharma Douglass Skinner, a great-great-great-great-grandchild of Douglass's, observes on camera after the readings:

> Someone once said that pessimism is a tool of white oppression, and I think that's true. I think in many ways we are still slaves to the notion that it will never get better. But I think that there is hope and I think it's important that we celebrate black joy and black life and we remember that change is possible, change is probable, and that there's hope.

I thought it had happened while I wasn't looking, but the moon is still huge; it's the only thing up there tonight. I must move to another window.

—July 5, 2020

(This essay is an expanded version of "We Must Act Out Our Freedom," *The New York Review of Books*, August 20, 2020.)

Notes

BLACKBALLED: THE BLACK VOTE AND US DEMOCRACY

1. Elizabeth Rauh Bethel, *Promiseland: A Century of Life in a Negro Community* (Temple University Press, 1981).

2. See also Cleveland Sellers, *The River of No Return: The Autobiography of a Black Militant and the Life and Death of SNCC* (Morrow, 1973). Sellers was jailed for six months in 1968 for inciting a riot, following disturbances at South Carolina State University in Orangeburg, South Carolina. Police fired into a crowd that was protesting segregation at a local bowling alley, killing three students and wounding twenty-seven others. Nine policemen were brought to trial and acquitted.

3. Manning Marable, *Black American Politics: From the Washington Marches to Jesse Jackson* (Verso, 1985); Barbara A. Reynolds, *Jesse Jackson: America's David* (JFJ Associates, 1985); Thomas Landess and Richard M. Quinn, *Jesse Jackson and the Politics of Race* (Jameson,

1985); *The New Black Vote: Politics and Power in Four American Cities*, edited by Rod Bush (Synthesis, 1984).

4. See also Richard Kluger, *Simple Justice: The History of Brown v. Board of Education and Black America's Struggle for Equality* (Knopf, 1975; 2004).

5. For a very different account of the FBI's attempts with the Justice Department to indict the killers of the four civil rights workers and the obstructionism of officials in Neshoba County, see Michal R. Belknap, *Federal Law and Southern Order: Racial Violence and Constitutional Conflict in the Post-Brown South* (University of Georgia Press, 1987).

6. David Remnick's *The Bridge: The Life and Rise of Barack Obama* (Knopf, 2010), as well as his profile of the president in *The New Yorker* (January 27, 2014), will likely remain for some time the most consulted biographical sources on a rather unknowable figure.

7. *The Texas Tribune*, February 26, 2014.

8. This view finds passionate expression in passages of Ronald Dworkin's *Freedom's Law: The Moral Reading of the American Constitution* (Harvard University Press, 1996).

9. See Gary May, *Bending Toward Justice: The Voting Rights Act and the Transformation of American Democracy* (Basic Books, 2013); Roy L. Brooks, *Racial Justice in the Age of Obama* (Princeton University Press, 2009); and Garrine P. Laney, *The Voting Rights Act of 1965: Historical Background and Current Issues* (Nova Science, 2003).

NOTES

10. "The Roberts Court v. Voting Rights," *The New York Review of Books*, April 4, 2013, and "Equality and the Roberts Court: Four Decisions," *The New York Review of Books*, August 15, 2013.

WHAT BLACK MEANS NOW

1. Zadie Smith, "Speaking in Tongues," *The New York Review of Books*, February 26, 2009, based on a lecture given at the New York Public Library in December 2008, and collected in *Changing My Mind: Occasional Essays* (Penguin, 2009).

2. See Bart Landry's *The New Black Middle Class* (University of California Press, 1987).

BUCK MOON IN HARLEM

1. The Texas-born black folklorist J. Mason Brewer published *Juneteenth*, a slim collection of folktales, in 1932. In a letter to Arna Bontemps, his coeditor of *The Book of Negro Folklore* (1958), Langston Hughes is pleased to have discovered *Juneteenth* in his research for their collection, noting that Brewer has the same alligator story as Bontemps, but his version is not as good. He has stories Hughes remembers having heard in his Kansas childhood but had since forgotten: "I ain't been there, but I been told bout how hit was in de slavery days." Brewer's tales of clever slaves in Hughes's volume are set on small

plantations along the Gulf and the Mexican border. See also *Juneteenth Texas: Essays in African-American Folklore*, edited by Francis Edward Abernethy and Carolyn Fiedler Satterwhite (University of North Texas Press, 1996). Ellison's literary executor, John F. Callahan, noted that his *Juneteenth* was drawn from a much longer and unfinished manuscript.

DARRYL PINCKNEY is the author of two novels, *High Cotton* and *Black Deutschland*, and two other works of nonfiction, *Out There: Mavericks of Black Literature* and *Busted in New York and Other Essays*.